Manchester Stories

THE AUTHOR

David Clayton was born in Withington Hospital and raised in Fallow-field and feels reasonably qualified to write this book having spent most of his life in Manchester. He began writing at a very early age and discovered English was the one subject he was good at. He loved making up stories, particularly historical and horror shorts, though it would be some time before he got paid for his efforts.

His first school was Mauldeth Road primary and he later went to Parrs Wood before doing a succession of jobs that he hated.

He began contributing to the official *Manchester City Magazine* in 1998 and wrote articles for free for a time. By then, with a work colleague, he had also launched *The Culture* – a fanzine on author Iain Banks. It proved to be a success, too, and got him a couple of paid jobs on *The Guardian* and so when the editor's job on the *City* magazine came up – it was then published by the *Manchester Evening News* group – he had amassed a decent portfolio and landed the job.

Clayton then started penning the odd book on football, almost always on City and later ghost-wrote the autobiographies of Shaun Goater and Ian Holloway, both of which were highly acclaimed. Turning his hand to the world of show-business, he also produced a biography of *Porridge* and *Rising Damp* star Richard Beckinsale.

After leaving the *Manchester Evening News* in 2009, he began working as a journalist at Manchester City FC, who at the time of writing, are still his employers.

These days he lives in Didsbury with his wife and children – two girls and one boy – and has no immediate plans to move away from a city that continues to fascinate him the more he learns about it.

Manchester Stories

David Clayton

Fort Publishing Ltd

First published in 2013 by Fort Publishing Ltd, Old Belmont House,
12 Robsland Avenue, Ayr, KA7 2RW

Cover design by Mark Blackadder

Typeset by 3btype.com

Printed by Bell and Bain Ltd, Glasgow

ISBN: 978-1-905769-41-4

This one is for my the people who have influenced me the most: my mum, Shirley Clayton, who represented Manchester as a roller-skater in the national championships; my sister, Wendy Howard; my wife Sarah and my children Harry, Jaime and Chrissie. It's also dedicated to the memory of my grandparents, Ernest and Maud Jackson, and my good friend Iain Banks.

CONTENTS

PREFACE

Writing a book about Manchester has been an ambition of mine for a long time. It's the city I've grown up and raised my family in and though there are moments when I wish I lived somewhere a little more rural, there is an undeniable attraction that always leaves me proud to be a Mancunian.

I grew up in Ladybarn, Fallowfield at a time when many of the local shops that were my world as a kid were beginning to close. They would eventually make way for new houses and a couple of supermarkets. Still, I'd got Maine Road when my mum could afford to take me and then wait for the *Football Pink* at the post office to see how the other teams had gone on.

It was a time when the *Manchester Evening News* was 'a friend dropping in', Alpine delivered a range of flavoured fizzy drinks once a week and a local man knocked on to collect the football pools. If I was really lucky, once a year we'd go to Belle Vue for the day – back when the city had its own zoo and theme park combined. Happy days!

In later years, when my writing career finally took off, I was based at the *Manchester Evening News* and I discovered the archives library where files lay on some of the city's most fascinating stories and characters.

The opportunity to write this book arose six years ago after I'd written a book for a publisher called Fort Publishing in Scotland. The company had done a number of similar books on cities and asked if I could produce a similar one for Manchester. I said I thought I could and embarked on the longest project I've ever worked on. I've been chipping away at it for what seems an age because the research demanded it and each time one story seemed to have reached its conclusion, another fascinating strand would develop and open a whole new area.

The eighteen stories inside these covers represent everything that makes Manchester great, iconic and dramatic. Each event, person or tragedy has become interwoven into the very fabric of the city and Mancunians have had their share of tragedies. And you don't have to scratch far beneath the surface of the fashionable suburbs to find a violent underbelly from years gone by. This is a tough, working-man's city and just over a century ago, the streets of Manchester were a place where you either sunk or swam.

There is a raft of books about the place that was once known as 'Cottonopolis', when Manchester became internationally renowned as the world's leading cotton and textile producer. Some individuals became fabulously wealthy and although they are long gone, the dark brooding mills that dot the city today are a constant reminder of our past.

The one thing I didn't want to do was recreate what others have done before me. I wanted to find stories that showed the best, and, on occasion, the worst of Mancunians. The people of this city are realists and will be the first to point out Manchester's faults, but there is also an understated pride and affection bubbling beneath the cynicism.

There are stories in this book that the reader will be familiar with, but there will be some that only the most ardent historians know of, and that's why writing about some of the people synonymous with Manchester was such as challenge.

Pat Phoenix was far more than just Elsie Tanner off *Coronation Street*, as you will discover, and Bernard Manning's rise to stardom is a tale of a man whose comedy simply caught up with him and all-but ended his television career as he became a figure of ridicule.

Then there is the shocking story of the Beast of Manchester and his terrible crimes that caused terror in the city for a time. We've had our tragedies, too, with the Woolworth's fire, the horrific plane inferno at Manchester Airport and the Collyhurst rail disaster. The Munich air tragedy has been covered in many books and documentaries, but how did the people of Manchester react in the days that followed? That has not been covered before and what happened in the aftermath of the crash shows the generosity of spirit of this remarkable city.

And Manchester once had its own film studios, known locally as Jollywood. Of all the stories in the pages that follow, my personal favourite is that of Jerome Caminada, our very own Sherlock Holmes who tracked down criminals by a variety of ingenious methods.

War, musicians, actors and even a pub that became a much-loved local landmark – before literally disappearing overnight – *Manchester Stories* has a bit of everything. Like the city itself.

David Clayton
Manchester
August 2013

1

'THE SEXIEST THING ON TELEVISION'

'You'll just have to bloody well guess, won't you?'

That wasn't the reaction producer Stuart Latham expected when he asked the struggling actress to take off her thick fur coat. After all, she was auditioning for a plum part, one that could make her a big star, and so it was important for him to have a look at her figure. Five thousand other hopefuls were desperate to appear in Granada's new television series so a little respect, maybe even a modicum of deference, would not have gone amiss.

One member of the auditioning panel, a blond-haired man of just twenty-three, didn't bat an eyelid at her reaction. In fact, it drew him to her. His name was Tony Warren and he was the writer and creator of the show, then called *Florizel Street*, but which would soon be known to the world as *Coronation Street*. He had searched high and low for his leading lady, spurning all those who had appeared before him. Then as Patricia Phoenix began to deliver the lines she had been given for the audition, Warren realised immediately that he had found his Elsie Tanner. This one, he thought, will do.

Warren was right. From the moment she first appeared on the small screen as Elsie, Phoenix was hypnotic as the flawed divorcée. She would provide the show's fire and brimstone for more than twenty years. Red-haired, resilient and stylish, it was little wonder that she became a beacon for downtrodden women and a sex symbol for millions of men. Such was her allure that Jim Callaghan, the former prime minister, proclaimed her 'the sexiest thing on television'.

For many, her character in the *Street* epitomised Northern resilience and warmth, but there was a steely resolve behind the knowing smile; nobody underestimated Elsie Tanner, not even battleaxe neighbour Ena Sharples and their numerous spats over the years became compulsive viewing. But once the cameras stopped rolling, where did Elsie Tanner end and Pat Phoenix begin? The dividing lines became blurred and as the years rolled by, it is fair to say that a majority of the soap's fans came to believe Pat and Elsie were one and the same.

Phoenix's background is almost as colourful as the character she ended up playing. The illegitimate daughter of a man a judge once described as 'a chivalrous bigamist', Patricia Frederica Manfield was born on 26 November 1923 at St Mary's hospital. Her parents, Anna Maria Noonan and Thomas Manfield, had married in a registry office. It was easy to see why she had fallen for Thomas: he had Latin good looks and an easy, roguish charm. He worked for a local newspaper on a range of promotions, a job that included playing the character of Percy Pickles. If a reader spotted 'Percy', who was always dressed in a natty suit and trilby, he or she could claim a cash reward from the paper. It wasn't the only part that Thomas Manfield played to perfection, because the moment the wedding ceremony was over, he had broken the law. He was still legally married to another woman.

That devastating fact would not come to light for many years and prior to the discovery, the family lived in a fine house on affluent Ducie Street in the centre of Manchester. During this period life was, Phoenix once said, 'one long Christmas'. It was a happy household and while there would occasionally be explosive arguments her parents were very much in love and disagreements invariably ended in fits of laughter. Patricia's father had a treasure trove of colourful stories, all made up for Patricia, who never tired of hearing them. Nothing was too good for his little daughter, the apple of his eye, and he lavished gifts on her all year round. He was the life and soul of the party and as Phoenix writes in her autobiography (*All My Burning Bridges*), 'When he laughs the world laughs,' although she later admits that 'the last laugh would be on my mother'.

Life was good, but Anna and Patricia's world was turned upside down when a policeman arrived at the family home and asked the question that shattered their lives.

'Do the Manfields live here?'

'Yes, why?' Anna replied.

'Because,' he said, 'Mr and Mrs Manfield are in hospital with injuries following a road accident.'

Anna informed the officer that he must be mistaken as *she* was Mrs Manfield. The house of cards so carefully constructed by Thomas Manfield had collapsed. He had indeed been involved in a car crash, but the woman injured in the accident was his lover, one of many casual affairs. When the story was reported in the press, his legal wife read the reports that her estranged husband had 'remarried', to Anna. He was duly prosecuted and the court gave him one day in prison. It was on the face of it a lenient sentence but the judge was impressed that Manfield had supported his wife financially for sixteen years and mitigated the punishment accordingly.

Anna did not feel the same way. Too proud to forgive her 'husband' for such dreadful deceit, she left the family home with her daughter to live with relatives several miles away. Despite several attempts by Manfield to run away with Patricia, Anna always stopped him and gradually he drifted out of their lives altogether.

It meant that in the eyes of the law, Patricia was illegitimate, not much of a problem in the twenty-first century but in the 1930s a source of shame. Her mother, however, refused to accept in the parlance of the day that her daughter was 'a bastard' and would point to her marriage certificate and to Patricia's birth certificate, both of which proved, in her eyes, that the birth had been entirely above board.

Anna later married painter and decorator Richard Pilkington and Patricia was raised as his daughter in Moss Side, close to Manchester City's Maine Road stadium. With her biological father banished from their lives, the domestic bliss she had known was gone forever. Her stepfather, a man scarred by the Great Depression of the 1930s, brought little happiness into Patricia's life as terrible arguments and physical abuse replaced laughter and excitement. Desperately unhappy, her mother told her, 'Don't ever get married. It's not worth the unhappiness.' Patricia never forgot those words, developing a deep distrust of men and commitment.

She attended the Fallowfield Central School for Girls, where a close friend was Betty Alberge, who would in time appear alongside her in *Coronation Street* as Florrie Lindley. Her passion for the performing arts was encouraged by teachers and away from the classroom she was drawn to the stage. She was a regular at the Palace Theatre, watching the likes of Laurence Olivier, Ralph Richardson, Sybil Thorndike and Michael Redgrave, dreaming of the day that she would tread the boards. Her first break came at the age of eleven, after she submitted a dramatic monologue to BBC Manchester about the death of Lady Jane Grey. The BBC was suitably impressed and invited the precocious schoolgirl to record her reading. As a result, she won a regular spot on the radio programme *Children's Hour*, which was then something of a national institution, particularly during wartime, when many youngsters were separated from their parents.

She continued to receive encouragement at school, too, and as one teacher wrote: 'Pat was not exactly a model pupil, but at the same time, on stage, she was just marvellous and I shall never forget her perform-ance as Tintagiles.' On leaving school, she worked briefly in a library before becoming a clerk for the gas board at Manchester town hall, while in the evenings she pursued her dream of working in the theatre. She joined an amateur dramatics group, progressing to the Manchester Arts Group and also attended various local repertory companies as she built up a body of work. In one group, run by James Lovell and Arthur Spreckley and based in Chorlton-cum-Hardy, she met the young Harry H. Corbett, destined for stardom in *Steptoe and Son*. Thanks to the newly formed Mancunian Film Studios, she won a part in the 1948 film *Cup-tie Honeymoon* alongside the popular music-hall comedian Sandy Powell, the man who dreamt up the catchphrase 'Can you hear me, mother?' She struck up a brief relationship with another actor, Tony Booth, while touring in the Somerset Maugham plays *Rain* and *A Girl Called Sadie*. Booth, however, was already married and both accepted it was no more than a fling at that point.

Not convinced her acting career was moving quickly enough, and bored by her job at the town hall, she dreamt of a life at sea and applied to join the WRENS, but her mother refused to sign the consent form and she had to rethink her plans. So it was back to acting and a spell at Joan Littlewood's theatre workshop at the Theatre Royal, Stratford

East led to minor roles in *Blood of the Vampire* and *Jack the Ripper* (both of which, incidentally, starred John Le Mesurier).

It was around this time that another very important man came into her life, or, to be more precise, came back into it. Pat was appearing in a play in Bramhall when a stage hand came into her dressing room and said there was a man waiting to see her. It was her father, whom she had not seen for twenty years. Tom Manfield told her he had remarried, to Lucy, and that they had two sons. He was now running a business, a florist and greengrocer shop in Walkden, and he seemed to be doing well. They kept in touch and when he died at the age of seventy-two, from lung cancer, she went to the funeral, although her mother refused to attend.

As repertory theatre began to decline and television took off in earnest, Pat Pilkington tried her luck in London, but the work was sporadic and eventually she tired of the business. Renting a seedy basement flat in Finsbury Park, with her career and personal life going nowhere (she was at this time separated from husband Peter Marsh, whom she had married in 1951) she decided, after much soul-searching, to end her life. Not wanting to upset her family, she planned her death to look like an accident. So, after preparing a cup of tea and putting the cat out, she lit a match, blew it out and then turned on the gas ring.

Fate, however, had other plans for Patricia Pilkington.

Awaking forty-five minutes later with a blinding headache, she discovered the reason she was still alive: the gas meter had run out! It was a pivotal moment and as she laughed at her own ineptness, she decided to give acting one last try. She sourced a new agent and sent in a curriculum vitae and photograph. When the agency called to say the ink on the back of her picture had smudged and could she spell out her name, she glanced down at a book she had been reading – *Phoenix Rising* – and adopted a new surname. Pat Pilkington became Pat Phoenix and it is hard to imagine a name she would have suited any better. After narrowly missing out on the lead role in the movie version of John Braine's best-selling and erotically charged novel *Room at the Top*, she won a summer-season contract in Blackpool, appearing with the great Thora Hird in *Happy Days*. After the run ended, Hird presented Pat with a bottle of champagne.

'Aren't you going to open it?' Thora asked.

'Not until I've made it,' Phoenix smiled.

Frustrated at not landing the kind of parts she felt she could play in her sleep, the 37-year-old returned to her home city, considering a life away from acting. The phone rarely rang and she would bemoan the fact that all she had to show for her years in rep was 'a broken marriage and no bank balance'. But things took an interesting twist when she was invited to take on the position of roving reporter on a lunchtime show, *People and Places*. She accepted and enjoyed the work immensely, and she also learned of auditions being held for a summer fill-in serial due to be filmed at Granada Studios in Manchester.

She wasn't the only one to harbour aspirations of television stardom. More than five thousand hopefuls applied and five hundred were seen, all with the dream of being cast in the thirteen-week drama. While most had little or no experience, a select few were head and shoulders above the rest, Pat Phoenix among them. When Tony Warren first set eyes on her at that now legendary audition, he was impressed not only by her testy response to producer Stuart Latham but also by her striking looks, and her fur coat. In those days, fur coats were the height of elegance and sophistication, not the objects of derision they are today. While he believed that in her mid-thirties Phoenix was ten years too young for the part, her pitch-perfect rendition of his script convinced him otherwise. She was also busty and glamorous, and, as Warren said, the woman playing Elsie Tanner had to be 'all tit and glitter'.

After winning the part, Pat Phoenix realised this was the break she had been looking for and that the role could give her the national exposure she craved. All she had to do was make a lasting impression. She had her work cut out as the *Street* was peppered with charismatic actresses who were all capable of stealing the show. Violet Carson was cast as Ena Sharples, Margot Bryant played the timid, sweet Minnie Caldwell; Doris Speed, the nearest thing the street had to royalty, played the landlady of the Rovers Return, Annie Walker, and Jean Alexander took on the role as Hilda Ogden. It was a fabulous cast by any standards.

Elsie Tanner was a new type of television character, a woman determined to enjoy life despite her humdrum existence, someone who couldn't have cared less what her neighbours, much less polite society, thought. She played the part with such conviction that for the watching millions, Pat Phoenix was Elsie Tanner. Her clashes with meddlesome neighbour Ena Sharples produced some of the most memorable scenes of *Coronation Street*'s first decade. The scripts were both sharp and down-to-earth and in the first episode, Phoenix's character was able to spout lines such as, 'Ee, Elsie, you're just about ready for the knacker yard,' and 'You're not a kid any more. It's no secret around here why your dad left me,' and 'Yer know, without a word of a lie, yer grandma Tanner were that bandy she couldn't have stopped a pig in an entry.'

Elsie Tanner's attitude to sex, and to men, was crucial and in its way groundbreaking. When we first meet her, she is separated from her seaman husband, Albert Tanner, and living with her ne'er-do-well son Dennis at 11 Coronation Street. What was shocking for some viewers was that she was one of the first female characters in British drama openly to entertain 'gentleman callers', the implication being that for her sexual intercourse outside of marriage was not that big a deal. Pat Phoenix instinctively 'got' Elsie and fully appreciated the importance of projecting a powerful sex appeal, memorably describing the woman she played as, 'The blousy, buxom sex bomb of the early sixties, satin blouses slashed at the neck, beads and tight black skirts.'

That understanding of what made her character tick, combined with a wonderful script, made her one of the biggest stars on television. That was perfectly illustrated when, in 1967, Elsie married for the second time. Her husband to be was Steve Tanner, a master sergeant in the US army. Elsie and Steve, quite unusually, had the same surname – Tanner. In fact this was testament to the crucial importance of the Elsie Tanner character to *Corrie*: when Steve Tanner was written out of the show, Elsie could keep calling herself Tanner.

However, it was the reaction of press and public to the wedding that showed the enormous hold *Coronation Street* and Elsie Tanner had on popular imagination. An astonishing twenty-one-million people tuned in to see the happy couple walk up the aisle, with a million buying a special souvenir edition of listings magazine *TV Times*. The episode was repeated, the first to get this treatment, and it became the template for showpiece weddings on television. Something else very interesting happened: it became apparent that a considerable number of viewers were confusing the fictional happenings in Weatherfield with real life.

Granada's staff were bemused when more than a thousand telegrams and letters arrived at the studios, all wishing the newlyweds well for the future while Elsie, much to the amusement of Pat Phoenix, got wedding presents from fans. Truth is indeed stranger than fiction.

Phoenix by now lived at 33 Epsom Mews, Higher Broughton, just two miles from Granada Studios, and despite her new-found wealth she kept her roots in Manchester and found the women of the city not only a constant inspiration but also a source of material for her character. Her private life was the subject of continual media scrutiny, although not quite the forensic examination the celebrities of today endure. In fact she had been in a relationship from the early days of *Coronation Street*, although it was not with someone in the business. At the age of nineteen she had met a young man by the name of Bill Nadin at a party. They began seeing each other and Nadin, as she puts it, took 'her virginity'. In such circumstances the honourable thing to do in those days was to marry the girl and Nadin did indeed make such an offer. Patricia's mother thought they were too young to make a commitment and the relationship withered on the vine.

It was not the end of the affair. Sixteen years after they first met, and at a time when she was at the peak of her popularity, he came back into her life. One day, no doubt rushing to get to get to rehearsals, she hailed a taxi. As the driver pulled up he said, 'I've been waiting sixteen years for this moment.' It was, of course, Bill and they picked up where they had left off, starting a new chapter in their lives. They would be together for eleven years and he also became her road manager, driving her to personal appearances up and down the country. When they did split up there was no animosity and the pair remained close friends.

With *Coronation Street*'s popularity peaking during the Seventies, Phoenix knew it was going to become increasingly difficult to live in Manchester and so she bought the eighteenth-century Sunny Side Cottage in Hollingworth, twelve miles from the city centre. Always approachable, she wasn't trying to get away from her legion of fans, but she needed space and the village of Hollingworth, close to Glossop and the foothills of the Pennines, offered her the chance to pop to the local shop for a pack of cigarettes and to live a relatively normal existence.

In 1972, she married Alan Browning (who played her third on-screen husband, Alan Howard, in *Coronation Street*) at Etherow Brow Methodist chapel in Broadbottom, close to her home. That was also the year Phoenix was the subject of *This Is Your Life* and she received the 'Big Red Book' on 15 November.

Coronation Street made Pat Phoenix rich and famous; with her house in Hollingworth being described as 'like something out of *Sunset Boulevard*' (a famous Hollywood film from 1950 in which Gloria Swanson's character lives in a palatial mansion). But the truth was she had begun to tire of the daily grind of rehearsals and of her character, telling friends that she 'was bored out of her mind playing Elsie'. She wanted to stretch herself as an actress. After all her reputation had been greatly enhanced by a part in the controversial 1962 film *The L-Shaped Room* in which she played Sonia, a prostitute, although the lead went to Leslie Caron. Perhaps she could paint on a bigger canvas.

There were other considerations. Freed from the requirement to pitch up every day at Granada she would be able to take on more advertising work and personal appearances, boosting her income but for considerably less effort. Another factor in her thinking could have been the atmosphere on set. The *Corrie* studios were not always the most harmonious, with Phoenix's own behaviour a factor. Stories did the rounds of her airs and graces, of her habit of bearing grudges, traits that did little to endear her to cast and crew.

Whatever the reasons, Pat Phoenix left *Coronation Street* in 1973. To no one's surprise ratings fell, although they were not helped by the temporary loss of that other female stalwart Ena Sharples, who had to be written out due to the ill health of Violet Carson. While away from the *Street*, Phoenix made a good living from theatre and commercial work, but it was perhaps not as lucrative or professionally rewarding as she had imagined.

Nor was her private life without its stresses and strains. The marriage to Browning was no bed of roses. He had a chronic drink problem, often polishing off two bottles of gin a day. Even when he 'stopped' drinking he would lace orange juice with alcohol and carry on regardless, while proclaiming to the world that he was on the wagon. Understandably, it affected their relationship. After five years, Pat Phoenix decided separation was the only answer and her mother's words of advice must have been ringing in her ears as her husband left the marital home for good.

Browning's drinking continued and it was only a matter of time before it killed him. In 1979 Pat was on holiday in Cornwall and got a call from Granada, who told her he was seriously ill. That night, she went out to dinner with friends, in Penzance, and when she went back to her rented cottage there were two cars waiting. It was the press.

'We'd like to know your reaction to Mr Browning's death?' one journalist asked.

It was a stunning blow.

'But I've been in touch with everybody this afternoon. Nobody said . . . I don't believe he's dead,' was her emotional response.

Despite the fact they had separated, Alan's death at the age of fifty-three was a massive blow. There had been genuine affection: 'I loved Alan, but he had a terrible disease. He was an alcoholic.'

Pat had gone back to the *Street* in 1976 and did her best to reinvigorate the character but some of the magic from the early days had gone. She again grew tired of Elsie while at the same time demanding an expensive wardrobe and scripts that would see her having romances with younger men. The producers considered both of these aspirations unrealistic, putting them at loggerheads with their biggest star. There was also dissatisfaction about money. She earned £25,000 a year at Granada, a salary that she compared, unfavourably, to the vastly bigger pay packets enjoyed by the stars of American soaps like *Dallas* and *Dynasty*. A second parting of the ways seemed inevitable and by 1984, unable to resolve her differences, she left *Coronation Street* for a second time, with viewers being told that Elsie had gone to run a wine bar in Portugal with her new screen husband, Bill Gregory.

Away from television she had at last found happiness. She rekindled her relationship with Tony Booth, whom she had remained fond of since the brief relationship some twenty-five years earlier. Booth – famous for his role as Alf Garnett's scouse son-in-law in *Till Death Us Do Part* – had suffered third-degree burns after a boozy escapade ended with a dreadful fire in which he was lucky to escape with his life. While convalescing at his mum's house, he sat watching an episode of *Coronation Street*, never thinking salvation was right in front of him.

In later years, he recalled how he became part of Phoenix's life once again.

> I was lost. I was staying with my mother, who knew I'd had a relationship with Pat, who was on TV at the time and said 'She's a very warm woman, maybe she can help you back into some kind of work.'
> My mum virtually dragged me to the phone to call her. Pat invited me over and was shocked at how I looked. I weighed only eight stone. We fell into each other's arms and were inseparable from then on.
> Pat was absolutely the most fantastic, vibrant woman I'd ever met in my life. Fate brought us together. Pat helped turn my life around.

Together from 1979 onwards, the pair planned to marry on a Trans-Siberian Express train journey, but work commitments got in the way and the pair continued their lives, blissfully happy.

The final break from *Corrie*, while undoubtedly a gamble, seemed to be paying off. She was still an idol to many, including, perhaps to her surprise, to the young and hip. The lead singer of Manchester band The Smiths, Morrissey, interviewed Phoenix, one of his heroines, for a magazine and would later use her image on the sleeve of the band's single 'Shakespeare's Sister', such was her iconic status. In terms of work there was no shortage of offers and she changed direction slightly after accepting TV-AM's proposal to become an agony aunt on their breakfast-television programme.

However, acting was her first love and she was soon cast in a play called *Hidden Talents*, taking the part of a woman dying of cancer, though nobody could have guessed how tragically prophetic the story-line would prove to be. In 1986, she won the lead in a sitcom, playing a Bridlington landlady in *Constant Hot Water*. By that time, however, as life imitated art, she was already suffering with advanced lung cancer. At Central Television's press launch for the series, Pat sat on a straight-backed chair while the assembled journalists gathered round for a question-and-answer session. She was asked if she was okay and she replied, 'Just a bit tired, that's all,' reassuring everyone with a trademark grin. As ever, she was the life and soul of the party, smiling and joking, looking as vibrant and stunning as ever though all the while she was exhausted and weak.

She was a pro to the last.

Gravely ill in August 1986, she was admitted to the private Alexandra hospital in Cheadle where she fought the disease with all the gusto she had put into her acting career. Alas, this was one battle she couldn't win. Despite the cancer, she said, 'At a time when I'm supposed to be all washed up and finished, I'm happier than I've ever been.' What she didn't tell anybody was that her condition was terminal.

With Tony Booth a constant companion during her time in hospital, the pair decided to do something they realised they should have done many years earlier. On 11 September 1986 her close friend, Father Charles Lynch – parish priest of Our Lady of Sorrows in Liverpool, and a close friend of Pat's – married the couple. It was not an easy ceremony to arrange. In those days licences to marry outwith a church or registrar's office were only issued in exceptional circumstances. Where the cause is due to illness, proof has to be provided that the patient cannot be moved and it was only when Phoenix's doctors furnished the necessary paperwork that the registrar general in London issued a special licence.

There was also the possibility that the Catholic Church might have refused to marry them, given that the bride-to-be had been hitched twice before. But as Father Lynch explained because her two previous marriages had been civil ceremonies 'in the eyes of the Church she had never been married'. There were only six people in the room when Tony Booth, 62, and Pat Phoenix, 54, finally tied the knot. For obvious reasons some traditions had to be ditched, so there was no best man or bridesmaids. But there was a link to her glory days: Tony Warren, who had always been close to his leading lady, was present.

Despite the circumstances – which also led to part of the last rites being administered – the priest thought it a happy occasion.

> It was a beautiful event, very tearful with lots of love. The room was heavy with emotion. Tony was crying and I had difficulty holding back my tears. Afterwards, Pat said she was ecstatically happy and Tony cried with joy. When I arrived at the hospital, Pat said, 'I want to make a dramatic exit.' I told her that she was going to make a graceful exit with all the sacraments of the Catholic Church.

Throughout her time in hospital, cards, letters and flowers poured in from well-wishers around the world and she even defied doctor's orders by holding a press conference to thank her fans because, 'People have been so wonderful.'

Sadly, just six days later, at 8.45 a.m. on 17 September, Pat Phoenix died peacefully in her sleep. There was not to be the wished-for dramatic exit, just a dignified passing, mourned by the nation.

'When we married, I didn't know she was going to die,' said Tony Booth. 'I hoped she was going to get better. Pat knew. It was heartbreaking, but she wanted to die as my wife.'

At the funeral, held a week later, her instructions were carried out to the letter, with a Roman Catholic requiem mass enlivened by a Dixieland jazz band and a black gospel group. The service was held at Holy Name church on Oxford Road, within sight of her birthplace, St Mary's hospital, and was conducted by two of Tony Booth's cousins: Father Paul Thomson and Father John Thomson. There was huge turnout, with five hundred mourners inside and more than a thousand outside listening to the mass on loudspeakers.

Coronation Street was well represented. Rehearsals had been cancelled for the day and this allowed seventeen members of the cast to go along and pay their respects. Tony Warren, of course, was in the church, along with *Corrie* executive producer Bill Podmore, chat-show host Russell Harty and Morrissey. Tony Booth's four daughters were there, including Cherie, accompanied by her husband, Tony Blair, who gave one of the readings. Mr Blair was described in the newspapers as 'MP for Sedgefield', but eleven years later would enter Downing Street as prime minister. To have been the stepmother of the wife of a Labour prime minister would have been a source of great pride for Pat Phoenix, who was a tireless worker for the party.

The service started with the coffin being carried into the church and onlookers noticed it was topped with a red and orange paper flower. The flower had been sent to Pat by a group of children who were also suffering from cancer. 'Put it on your wedding cake,' the big-hearted, and courageous, kids told her.

It was a poignant, yet often joyous, occasion, just what Pat would have wanted. In his eulogy Father Paul Thomson paid tribute to her courage and thanked God for her talent in 'capturing and reflecting the joys and sorrows of life in the north of England'. As the coffin left the church, the band played 'When the Saints Go Marching In', just as she had requested. Julie Goodyear, who played Bet Lynch in the long-running soap, perfectly summed up the mood of the mourners: 'Knowing Pat, I'm sure it was just the sort of send off she would have wanted. It was a belter.' After a cremation at Southern cemetery, Booth took his wife's ashes and buried them at their home in Hollingworth.

In her 1974 autobiography *All My Burning Bridges*, Pat observes, 'My father, who smoked Woodbines all his life, died of lung cancer at the age of seventy-two saying he was too young to die. And he was.' So was she.

Without doubt one of Manchester's favourite daughters, her name lived on in the form of a successful £1 million cancer appeal for Wythenshawe hospital. In so many ways, Pat Phoenix proudly represented the city and its people on screen for almost twenty-five years.

It is hard to imagine a better ambassador.

2

HITLER'S CHRISTMAS BLITZ

Manchester was looking forward to Christmas. It was December 1940 and after fifteen months of gruelling all-out war against Germany people of all ages hoped for a little respite. A normal festive season was out of the question, simply because these were far from normal times: thousands of favourite sons were in uniform, many of them overseas; rationing had been imposed; the city, with its nightly blackouts and anti-aircraft emplacements, resembled an armed camp. Nevertheless people would do their best, especially for the children, whose young lives had been blighted beyond all recognition.

There were some signs of normality. Halfway through December, Christmas shopping was in full swing as people flocked to the shops in Deansgate and Piccadilly. The theatres were advertising their pantomimes: at the Manchester Opera House, Britain's most famous comedian, Tommy Trinder, was appearing as Buttons in *Cinderella*, while at the Palace a cast including Leslie Henson and Stanley Holloway were staging *Robinson Crusoe*. Football fans also had something to cheer about: although official English league matches had been put in cold storage for the duration of the war, professional football was kept alive in the shape of the North Regional tournament; Manchester United fans looked forward to the visit of Stockport County while those of a light-blue persuasion were making plans for City's trip to Burnley.

Maybe, Manchester thought, it won't be too bad; we might be able to enjoy Christmas. Unfortunately, Adolf Hitler had other ideas.

The bombing campaign that became known as the Blitz started in August 1940. At that time, the RAF and the Luftwaffe were engaged in a fight to the death for dominance of the skies above southern England, a fight that became known as the Battle of Britain. Hitler's aim in unleashing the Blitz was to use Germany's bombers to destroy the capacity of British industry to provide the RAF with new planes. When he achieved air superiority, the Fuhrer intended to mount Operation Sealion – the invasion of Britain. Of course the Luftwaffe never did achieve air superiority but that did not mean ending the Blitz. If anything it grew more intense as the Germans took the view that they could bomb this country into submission by destroying our productive capacity and, at the same time, terrorising the populace. The Blitz would last for ten long months, ending only in May 1941.

As the leading industrial city in Britain, Manchester, with its engineering works, munitions factories, warehouses and railway yards, was a crucial target for the Luftwaffe. And so it proved. In both August and October 1940, Manchester felt the full force of Hitler's onslaught. But that was just the warm-up. The main show was yet to come and it came as the festive season was getting into full swing. The nights of 22/23 and 23/24 December 1940 wreaked utter havoc on the city. During the first night, the *Manchester Evening News* reported that, 'Hospitals, shops, houses and commercial buildings were destroyed' by the 370 German planes that took part in the raid. The next instalment, just twenty-four hours later, was, as the *Manchester Evening Chronicle* records, even more destructive.

> Manchester had its longest and most severe aerial bombardment last night and after twelve hours' blitz a pall of smoke hung over the city today. A church and other historic buildings were damaged. Wave after wave of planes roared over the city every few minutes and targets for the later arrivals were made with the fires that were started. Some of the fires cast a deep red glow in the sky, which was visible for miles.

The Luftwaffe's aim was to cause as much devastation as possible and to do so there was widespread use of the incendiary bomb. About a foot long, and two inches in diameter, they were packed thirty-six to a canister, which would burst open on release from the aircraft, scattering the incendiaries over a wide area. It is estimated that no less than 37,000 of these deadly devices were dropped on Manchester on the night of 22/23 December, along with nearly three hundred tons of high-explosive bombs. The incendiaries not only set off fires but also lit up the night sky, making it easier for later waves of bombers to find their targets with high explosives. The raiders were also guided by the fires that were still burning in Liverpool from raids that had started two nights' earlier.

The city centre sustained heavy damage as many of the best-known buildings took direct hits and immediately caught fire. Indeed the damage was so severe that the government – using the emergency censorship laws of the time – banned newspapers from publishing photographs of the aftermath. It was only months later that people were allowed to see images of the devastated Victoria and Exchange stations and the pile of rubble that was the Shambles, one of Manchester's oldest shopping centres. The Free Trade Hall was reduced to a pile of rubble, leaving the Hallé Orchestra homeless and forced to take up residence at the King's Hall, Belle Vue. Other notable buildings destroyed included Cheetham's Hospital, the Corn Exchange, Smithfield Market, the Gaiety Theatre and St Anne's church. The only slight consolation was that anti-aircraft guns had managed to bring down a German bomber in the skies above Old Trafford.

If incendiary and high-explosive bombs were not bad enough, the Germans used an even more deadly weapon against Manchester: the parachute mine. On the night of 22/23 December, the Luftwaffe deployed eighteen Heinkel 111s, each carrying two parachute mines. Because of their much slower rate of descent, the mines had deadly potential. The idea was that they would land in the street, roll over and then detonate, occasioning considerably more damage than conventional bombs, which buried themselves twenty feet underground before going off. Some of the mines failed to explode, like the one that went through the roof of 32 Dulcie Street in Chorlton-on-Medlock, where it finished up in the cellar. Others did go off, often to deadly effect, as Irene Pope told the *Manchester Evening News* many years later.

> We lived in Trafford Street, Salford and our yard backed onto the yard of St Bartholomew's school and we had brick air-raid shelters built round the outside toilets. My mother, gran, granddad and myself went into the shelter when the sirens sounded, but, during a lull in the Blitz, the ladies went into the yard to enable granddad to use the toilet in privacy, when suddenly this mine came floating over the school yard.

It was losing height but we realised it was heading for the houses next to ours, which had attics, so they were a storey higher than ours.

Suddenly, a gust of wind came. It seemed to twist the parachute and took the mine over our house, missing the next one literally by inches. But the tragic result was that it lost height when it reached Ordsall Lane and landed on an ARP post, killing all the wardens, who were colleagues of my father. He himself was an air-raid warden, but at the time was at another post.

A parachute mine also landed on a chimney at Manchester Royal Infirmary. Still attached to its parachute it didn't go off, but when Hugh Varah of the Auxiliary Fire Service got there he was faced with the possibility of the mine falling out of the parachute, rolling over and obliterating the entire building. After helping several nurses to get out – the hospital had already been damaged by high explosives – Varah remembered a nurse he had seen lying on the floor of a ward. At the time, he had assumed she was dead but now he asked himself if she had just passed out. Could she really still be alive?

Like many other ordinary people that night, Hugh Varah displayed extraordinary courage. In spite of the unexploded mine, he dashed back upstairs to the ward, grabbed a stethoscope from a drawer, ripped open the nurse's uniform and listened. In an instant he heard the unmistakeable sound of a human heart, beating fast. With the assistance of a policeman, Varah hurriedly put together a makeshift sling and between them they managed to lower the stricken woman to the ground floor. It was only then that the cause of the nurse's collapse became clear, as Varah explains.

> Just then it came to me what her problem was. That curious smell. She had sugar diabetes. And she was in a coma. I recognised the smell from an infirmary where I'd spent time in my younger days. I told the stretcher men and they looked at me:
> 'Don't you worry, doc. We'll see that they take notice.'
> And off they went.

As the bombardment continued, there were, inevitably, some horrific sights. Books on the London blitz relate how people were found hanging from wires on the underground, minus one or more of their limbs. It was the same in Manchester. And once again fireman Hugh Varah was a witness to what happened in one such incident.

I arrived at London Road station in Manchester in the middle of a raid. We were told to take cover. I thought the best thing to do was to marshal the other passengers and keep them alongside the thick brick wall. I got them nicely settled, some sitting, some crouching but one man dashed down the slope. He was trying to cross the road to reach an air-raid shelter that he said was up a side street. He arrived at the bottom of a slope at the same time as a falling bomb.

If I close my eyes I can still see his head come bowling back up the slope, like a hairy football.

(Both Varah incidents quoted in *Forgotten Voices of the Blitz and the Battle for Britain*, Joshua Levine, 2006.)

*

The scale of the German attacks on those two terrible nights was bad enough. However, to make matters worse, two hundred of Manchester's firemen and thirty pumps had been sent to help out in Liverpool, where the German attacks had started a little earlier. Those who were left plunged straight into the inferno, where they faced an additional and quite unexpected hazard. In a tactic that showed their utter contempt for human life the German planes swooped low and tried to machinegun those desperately trying to douse the flames.

However, if the Luftwaffe thought it would deter the gallant fire-fighters and civil-defence workers they were very much mistaken. By the second night – now assisted by crews returning from Liverpool and reinforcements from all over the north of England – the Manchester brigade and the Auxiliary Fire Service, the AFS, managed to get most of the fires under control. It was a heroic effort, simply because of the scale of the operation. No less than four hundred separate fires, a hundred of them in the serious category, had broken out. Many roads were blocked by falling debris, making it very hard or even impossible to get to fires. In some cases, difficult decisions had to be made: to prevent fires spreading in built-up areas, streets were cleared and buildings dynamited.

The people of Manchester responded magnificently. Men dashed out into the street, without a thought for their own safety, and did their best to douse the flames with sand. Nurses and other medical staff were especially brave. As we have seen, Manchester Royal Infirmary took several direct hits but amid the carnage the *Chronicle* noted that 'nurses worked heroically and heedless of the danger as bombs dropped around them'. Indeed the damage was so bad that at one point it was thought that the Royal would have to be evacuated.

The women of Manchester, like their menfolk, responded magnificently. In an article by a 'Woman Reporter' on 23 December, the *Chronicle* vividly describes their defiant attitude to the raids.

> Northern business girls know to how to take an air raid. A couple of aspirins the morning after and they carry on, even if it means, as it did in Manchester this morning, walking miles from their homes to their places of work, or begging lifts on the backs of lorries.
>
> Half-ashamed of being a few minutes late, shop-girls arriving before their chief found their way into the premises through broken windows and immediately began clearing all rescue-able stocks which had been on display. Others, whose normal job concerned expensive model fashion wear, grabbed brooms and assisted in sweeping up glass fragments.

The public was also keen to get back to normal as quickly as possible, especially as there was unfinished business to attend to: 'Customers wandered in to complete Christmas shopping purchases just as they had done in times of peace.'

As in the rest of Britain, Mancunians were forced to seek refuge in bomb shelters. The *Manchester Evening Chronicle* reported on one such shelter in Arundel Street, Hulme, noting that it was 'clean and well-aired' with 'many bunks'. The Christmas spirit was evident, as mothers used their precious sugar and butter rations to make Christmas treats for 'the little ones'. Parents were determined to ensure that their children had a good time and they even put up a Christmas tree, under which a huge pile of presents was visible. While on the wall of the shelter someone had pinned up a highly appropriate verse.

Kindness is forgetting self
Remembering others' needs,
The giving of encouragement
By helpful words and deeds.

While people may have been relatively safe in the shelters, their homes were a different matter. Eight thousand domestic dwellings were either destroyed, or rendered uninhabitable. The authorities immediately set about organising temporary accommodation and within two days of the raids twenty-five refuges had been opened. Lord Mayor R. G. Edwards made a tour of the shelters and pronounced himself, 'profoundly impressed by the way in which the citizens have faced the ordeal through which they have passed. Manchester said it could keep up its chin and it is doing so.'

Despite losing all their possessions, including their houses, the residents of the temporary shelters did their best to keep up morale. Manchester's famous Wood Street Mission was home to dozens of displaced people, ranging from 8-month-old baby Hanny to 73-year-old Mary Ellis. According to a newspaper reporter, the ordeal they had suffered had done little to dent their optimism: 'Such is the spirit of these homeless people that even had they been Christmas partying they could not have been a much cheerier crowd.' Special consideration, as always, was extended to the young ones: 'The kiddies, many of them scantily dressed, were having a really gay and noisy time between biscuits and tea, despite the fact that most of them had not had any sleep throughout the twelve-hour blitz.'

While the vast majority of Mancunians responded magnificently some people – a very small minority – blotted their copybook. Looting was a problem in the city, as it was throughout Britain. The damage to shops made it just too tempting for those with loose fingers. On 24 December four men were up before Manchester magistrates on looting charges. Among them was Edmund Ford, a 40-year-old from Fallow-field, who had stolen a metal cigarette case valued at 15s 6d from a tobacconist's window. A Sergeant Bailey of Manchester police told the court that he 'saw Ford with his hand through the bomb-shattered window, placing something in his overcoat pocket. I grabbed his hand and found this metal cigarette case in it. When I accused him of stealing it, he said "I can't remember whether I took it or not".' Ford was remanded in custody.

If they were found guilty, looters got much more than just a slap on the wrist. On 27 December, labourer Patrick Petersen, a Manchester man and also aged forty, tearfully pleaded guilty to stealing an enamel kettle from a damaged shop and got four months in jail. 'I cannot do my duty unless I deal with this class of case very severely,' the magistrate, in his sternest tones, told Petersen. Nor was it just members of the public who were unable to resist temptation. On New Year's Eve, two soldiers and an auxiliary fireman were sent to prison at Manchester city police court for looting from damaged shops while an air raid was in progress, a raid they were meant to be protecting the public from.

Looters imprisoned, fires extinguished, rubble cleared, roads reopened. By 27 December, Manchester was starting to get back to some kind of normality. There was just one more thing that had to be done. And it was the most heartrending task of all. Burying the dead.

Along with all the houses that had been damaged or destroyed – many of them in Salford – an estimated 684 people had been killed and a further 2,364 wounded. It was a traumatic experience for the relatives of the missing; most of them didn't know if their loved ones were in hospital, trapped below rubble or dead. Given the sheer scale of the casualties, the authorities instructed people looking for news not to go to the mortuaries and hospitals. Instead they were told to look at the lists on the public notice boards or to go along to a temporary casualty bureau, which had been set up in room 324 of the town-hall extension. It may have been impersonal, even callous, but, given the chaos into which the city had sunk, there was probably no alternative.

What followed was even more poignant. On 28 December, hundreds of the dead, covered only by a cheap shroud, were buried in a mass grave at Manchester's Southern Cemetery. Strenuous efforts were made to make the ceremony as dignified as possible. The 'Last Post' was played, wreaths were laid on behalf the city, the fire brigade and other civil-defence organisations and many dignitaries including the Lord Mayor were present. Nevertheless it must have been hard to take for those who had been bereaved, not knowing which of the shrouds contained the remains of their loved one. It was a scene repeated all over Britain as the authorities struggled to cope with burials on an industrial scale.

Dignity, stoicism and making the best of a bad job. That is the picture that is usually painted of behaviour on the home front during the war. Some historians, however, have argued that British defiance in the face of the Blitz, the famous stiff upper lip portrayed in newspapers and movies, was in fact a myth. They point out that there was strict censorship during the war and that the media were expected to do their bit by writing only positive stories. This extract, written by journalist Cyril Dunn on the morning after one of the raids on Manchester, appears to confirm this contention.

> There were big fires everywhere, the air stank of smoke and the streets were full of black ash as if there'd been a volcanic eruption. The destruction was enormous and spectacular, but it's ceased to make any impression on me. Even to see the whole of the Royal Exchange gutted and burning, whacking great buildings blasted into ruins, water spurting into the road from burst mains; the cathedral, shattered glass everywhere like dirty drifts of pack ice – this scarcely interested me.
>
> I went around nervously collecting the same old stories. 'All I want to do,' said one publican, who'd been blasted out of his cellar 'is to get out of here and stop out. I've had enough.' And a woman: 'If only I could feel it was worth it, was helping to win the war. But this [the ruins of her pub] is everything we've worked for.'
>
> I wrote the usual story about the cheerful courage and determined endurance of the Manchester folk.

There is no doubt some truth in this analysis. Many residents of our big cities lost everything they had, including their houses. Others were understandably terrified by the death and destruction all around them. The scenes in central Manchester during the Christmas of 1940 would have dismayed even the most philosophical among us. It is also likely that people were likely to be more negative if they were interviewed the morning after a raid, and the publican and the woman mentioned above fall into that category. It is hard to put on a brave face when you are standing amongst the smouldering remains of your home or business.

The fact is that Hitler's plan to cripple Britain's industrial capacity did not work. This country, including Manchester, continued to churn out planes, ships, guns and ammunition, all vital to the war effort. Nor did the Fuhrer manage to crush the spirit of the British people. If anything their resolve was hardened by the Blitz, their will to win enhanced. We need only look at the response from Manchester's firemen. In the aftermath of the raids, Manchester's Chief Constable John Maxwell compiled a report on how the city's fire brigade and civil defences had coped. It is an official document, sober in tone and wholly objective. Maxwell was neither a journalist nor a propagandist. He was a hard-headed and pragmatic senior policeman. Yet he could not conceal his great admiration for those who had risked their lives to bring the conflagration under control. Observing that twelve firemen lost their lives, Maxwell writes: 'Although themselves exhausted to the point of collapse, the senior officers rallied the men to combat the giant menace and the men, despite their fatigue, attacked the fires with amazing vigour and spirit.' Moreover, he goes on, they were successful because 'within a few hours of the termination of the raids all fires were under complete control'.

'Amazing vigour and spirit'. Those were the qualities displayed by the people of Manchester as they did everything in their power to defeat the evil creed of National Socialism. It was summed up admirably by doughty old Mary Ellis, who had lost everything and was forced to spend Christmas with dozens of other lost souls in the Wood Street Mission.

'It'll take more than Hitler to get us down.'

3

AND THE ACADEMY AWARD FOR BEST ACTOR GOES TO . . .

The stage was set. At the glittering ceremony in Los Angeles, the biggest movie star on the planet was about to win the Oscar for best actor. After a career-defining performance in the most lucrative box-office smash in history nothing could stop Clark Gable, the King of Hollywood, from lifting that precious gold statuette. Nothing, that is, apart from a modest, yet supremely talented, actor from Manchester.

The scene was the twelfth Academy Awards ceremony, hosted by Bob Hope. This was the Golden Age of Hollywood and that was reflected in the films the Academy voters had to choose from. It was an exceptional collection by any standards. Among the releases under consideration were *The Wizard of Oz* (starring Judy Garland), *Stagecoach* (John Wayne), *Beau Geste* (Gary Cooper and Ray Milland), *Of Mice and Men* (Lon Chaney and Burgess Meredith), *The Private Lives of Elizabeth and Essex* (Errol Flynn and Bette Davis) and *Ninotchka* (Greta Garbo). According to one eminent film historian, that year of 1939 'produced more bona fide classics than any similar period in moviemaking annals'.

It was a stellar list but one movie seemed certain to eclipse them all: *Gone with the Wind*, based on Margaret Mitchell's novel of the same name. The book had not only been a huge bestseller but had also won its author the prestigious Pulitzer Prize for fiction and in the process had captured the imagination of America. It was therefore inevitable that everything surrounding the making of the film version would be headline news: the casting; the choice of director; the budget, which at $4 million was huge by the standards of the time. It is no exaggeration to state that *Gone with the Wind* was the most anticipated film of all time.

The cast was top notch. Leslie Howard, Olivia de Havilland, Vivien Leigh; and at its head Gable, the biggest star in the firmament and the first choice of everyone who counted to play the lead role of Rhett Butler. Already the winner of the 1934 best-actor Oscar for *It Happened One Night* there was a general feeling that a second accolade was his for the asking. *Gone with the Wind* was certainly on a roll, winning an unprecedented eight Oscars including the awards for best film, best director and best actress. Movie fans around the world fully expected Gable to leave the ceremony that night clutching his second statuette.

They were to be disappointed. Because, as the saying goes, the Academy Award for best actor went to . . . Robert Donat for his performance in *Goodbye Mr Chips*. Although he had not been the favourite to win, it was no fluke. Donat was a superb, and subtle, actor, who radiated warmth from every pore. Nor was it a flash in the pan. He had been nominated before, for *The Citadel*, when he lost out to the man many well-informed critics believe was the greatest movie actor of all time: Spencer Tracy. Donat faced stiff competition for his Oscar. In addition to Gable he had been up against James Stewart, Mickey Rooney and the peerless Laurence Olivier. Intriguingly, the Academy's verdict came as no surprise to one of its distinguished members: Clark Gable. That was because the *Los Angeles Times* came out at 8.45 p.m. and took a decision to reveal the names of the winners, including of course Donat. Much to the annoyance of the organisers, the paper had jumped the gun and never again would journalists be entrusted with advance information about the Oscars.

So how did the man from Manchester manage to climb the greasy pole that was Hollywood success, in the process surpassing some of the greatest names in the business? There was no showbiz tradition in his family, nor were the Donats wealthy or well-connected. Robert had to rely on talent, hard work and sheer perseverance for his day in the sun.

He was born in March 1905, the youngest of four brothers, and was christened Frederick Robert Donat by his parents. His father, Ernst Donat, was an immigrant from Poland, a university-educated engineer.

Like many thousands of others he had come to Manchester to make his living in the textile industry, in his case as the representative of a cotton-spindle company based in Germany. While in England, Ernst met Rose Green, from Yorkshire, and they later married. As Robert was growing up, the family lived in St Paul's Road, Withington and after a spell at a local nursery he was sent to Ducie Avenue Central School in Ardwick.

Robert was fascinated by Manchester's trams and would remember them fondly for his whole life. His house was near to the West Didsbury line and as an infant he would race them on his tricycle, while later they would be the preferred mode of transport to school. In the mornings, from the tram window, he would see the distinctive figure of C. P. Scott pedalling furiously on his way to the *Manchester Guardian*'s offices in the city centre. The boy discovered that the elderly, bearded man on the bicycle was the editor of that distinguished organ and from that day on referred to Scott as 'our greatest townsman'.

In 1916, after his primary education was complete, he was sent to the Central High School for Boys, which in normal times held classes in Whitworth Street. Due to the war, however, the building had been commandeered for use as a hospital so for the duration of the conflict Robert and his classmates were farmed out to temporary classrooms all over the city. It was no bed of roses. He was by no means a great scholar and as well as being asthmatic had the added disadvantage of a bad stammer, something that one teacher in particular mercilessly mocked him for. Yet he found in his alma mater – as so many successful people do – an inspirational teacher: J. G. Birkby, 'Birkos' to his pupils. Birkby's enthusiasm for the arts in general, and theatre and opera in particular, rubbed off on Robert Donat. It proved to be a lifelong friendship because the two men, master and pupil, would correspond regularly down the years. Apart from anything else, Donat was always keen to hear the news from his home city of Manchester and Birko no doubt kept him up to date on that score.

Although Robert, like most boys of the time, was attracted to the new phenomenon of the cinema it is difficult to explain where his love for the theatre and acting came from. According to his mother he was 'stage struck' from the age of seven or eight. It certainly didn't run in the family; neither of his parents had even a remote connection with that world and when they were old enough his three big brothers would be packed off to Canada to make a life for themselves in the more mundane world of farming. Yet here was Robert, still at primary school, writing, directing and acting in little plays in the tool-shed in the back garden. He was always active, always on the move, despite the asthma, a condition that would prove to be a lifelong affliction.

The reaction of his parents to the young thespian in their midst was mixed. They did not approve of the movies, which they considered to be less than respectable entertainment. The stage, with its Shakespearean traditions, was a different matter. Here was a noble calling in which their young son might one day make a living. Ernst foresaw two potential problems: Robert had a thick Lancashire accent and a pronounced stammer, creases that would have to be ironed out if his son was to tread the boards. So his father sent him to study with James Bernard at his Fallowfield studios. Bernard – 'BB' to his close friends – was an elocution teacher who also put on productions of popular plays and books like *A Christmas Carol* and *Twelfth Night*.

Bernard recognised Robert's talent right from the word go: his natural quality on stage, his poise, his amazing facility at learning lines. A highly professional and demanding teacher, BB taught his young charge the rudiments of acting and stagecraft and soon they were appearing together at recitals all over the north-west, in church halls and school gymnasiums. On the way home from performances Robert found another use for his beloved trams: as one passed, he would use the noise to muffle the sound of him declaiming lines from Shakespeare and Dickens.

The young man had no money to pay for his acting and elocution lessons but, luckily for him, Bernard accepted payment-in-kind: Robert did secretarial work around the studio, an informal arrangement that developed into a full-time job when he left school at the age of fifteen. BB, however, knew that his protégé was destined for greater things and was determined to give him a leg-up. He introduced Robert to two of the leading actor-managers: Sir Frank Benson and Henry Baynton. In 1921 it led to Donat's first professional engagement, with the Baynton touring company at the Prince of Wales theatre in Birmingham. At the age of just sixteen he played a number of Shakespearean parts and when the summer season was over it was back to Fallowfield and his secretarial duties.

The theatre was now his life. He continued to work with BB, was a regular at plays staged by Manchester Opera House and travelled as often as he could to the West End of London to see the latest productions. His work in repertory theatre continued throughout the 1920s: with Frank Benson; with Alfred Wareing at the Theatre Royal, Huddersfield; with the Festival Theatre, Cambridge, which featured classics from the modern British and European repertoire. This provided Donat with a wide variety of challenging roles, experiences that would stand him in good stead as his career progressed. He even found time to get married, to Ella Voysey, a union that at produced two sons and a daughter, although it would ultimately end in divorce.

The role that propelled him to prominence was Gideon Sarn in *Precious Bane*, a play by Mary Webb. After the first night, which was in the West End, the audience was so enthralled by his virtuosity that they chanted 'Donat, Donat'. His performance did not go unnoticed by film producers in Britain, or by those across the Atlantic. He received a cable from the legendary Hollywood producer, Irving Thalberg, offering him the male lead alongside Norma Shearer in the film *Smilin' Through*. However, such was his love of theatre that he turned Thalberg down, opting to sign a contract with Alexander Korda's London Films, a move that allowed him to combine movies with the theatre. He built his film portfolio with parts such as Thomas Culpepper in *The Private Life of Henry VIII* and as the title character in *The Count of Monte Cristo*, the latter role leading many critics to hail him as the new Clark Gable or Douglas Fairbanks.

These movies were, however, but an appetiser. The main course was yet to come: a trio of parts that would elevate him into the ranks of the superstar. The first was *The Thirty-Nine Steps*, based on the best-selling novel of the same name by John Buchan and released in 1935. Produced by Korda and directed by Alfred Hitchcock, it follows the fortunes of hero Richard Hannay as he tries to prevent an organisation called the Thirty-Nine Steps from stealing British state secrets. The film is full of cliff-hangers but despite being a thriller it has many comic moments. Donat was perfect for the part, switching effortlessly from action sequences to light comedy.

Another important factor was the screen chemistry between him and leading lady Madeleine Carroll, a cool blonde. It was sizzling. Hitchcock pulled out all the stops to ratchet up the sexual tension. One scene called for Donat and Carroll to be handcuffed together and after they had acted it out, Hitch 'lost' the key to the cuffs and they were bound to each other for another hour before he 'found' it and freed them. The great director's ploy worked beautifully, both on and off screen, with Donat later confessing to a torrid affair with Carroll, despite him being married with children. It all helped and the film became a huge hit worldwide.

The middle leg of the trio was 1938's *The Citadel*, based on the book by A. J. Cronin. Donat plays Dr Manson, who, when we first meet him, is a newly qualified doctor from Scotland ministering to the miners of south Wales. Later Manson abandons this pioneering work for a lucrative private practice in Mayfair. Therefore in the course of the film the character not only ages considerably – requiring Donat to play a man several decades older than himself – but also becomes a different person, changing from a young idealist into a cynical sophisticate. He rose magnificently to the challenge and for good measure observers praised his near perfect Scottish accent. In fact his powerful portrayal of Manson won him an Academy Award nomination for best actor. He did not win the Oscar, losing out to Spencer Tracy, although it may have been some consolation when he received a telegram from Los Angeles, congratulating him on his fine performance.

> Mr Donat, I wish I could adequately express to you how deeply your Manson in *The Citadel* has impressed me. It is beautiful. I shall remember it always. Sincerely, Spencer Tracy.

The final work in the pantheon was of course *Goodbye Mr Chips*. Once again Donat not only had to age considerably but also to play a man whose personality completely changes over the years: in the film the main protagonist, Mr Chipping, or Chips, goes from a dull, unpopular schoolmaster to a benevolent and much-loved old man. It was an interesting and demanding part, enhanced by the prospect of working alongside an exceptionally strong supporting cast: Greer Garson played his wife, John Mills was one of his pupils and it also featured Paul Henreid, who later appeared in *Casablanca*. Despite this, many of Donat's friends advised him not to take the part, believing it would conflict with his image as the dashing leading man. They were wrong. *Chips* was a triumph, leading him to the Oscar that had so narrowly eluded him for *The Citadel*.

It was a popular, and much-merited, win. James Stewart, who knew a thing or two about screen acting, said that 'Every screen actor in the world should go and study Robert Donat as Mr Chips. There is something so magnificent in this character study and performance that it seems almost a miracle that it could happen.' Paul Muni, considered the greatest character actor in movies, agreed: 'That is the most magnificent performance I've seen on any screen.' While Samuel Goldwyn, the most powerful producer in Tinsel Town, was equally enthusiastic: 'It was nothing short of inspirational . . . not only for yourself . . . but for all of us who are part of the motion-picture industry.' The accolades from his peers meant the world to him, although the same cannot be said of his attitude to the gold statuette itself – he used it to prop open the bathroom door in his house.

Thus honoured, and a huge draw at the box office, there is no doubt that Donat could have been a giant in Hollywood. It was his for the taking. He had the looks, the talent and the star quality. Four factors prevented it: his ongoing problems with asthma, which led to his missing out on several meaty roles; his desire to keep performing in the English theatre; his disdain for the scrutiny fame of that magnitude would have brought in its wake; the nature of many of the roles he was offered (Robin Hood, Captain Blood and the like), which would have typecast him as the swashbuckling hero. So he continued to mix films with treading the boards and was much praised in the latter capacity for his Benedick in *Much Ado about Nothing* and as Thomas Becket in T. S. Eliot's *Murder in the Cathedral*.

He was of course by no means perfect. Despite his marriage to Ella he had a string of lovers, including most of his leading ladies. He carefully recorded details of the affairs, something that came to light after his death. One actress he did not sleep with was Marlene Dietrich, his co-star in *Knight Without Armour*, made in Britain by Alexander Korda. La Dietrich arrived in London to shoot the film – along with no less than thirty-six suitcases – on the lookout for a new beau after her previous relationship with fellow Hollywood superstar John Gilbert had broken down. Donat, she thought, would be ideal and so she invited him to her suite at Claridge's. He was so flustered by the attentions of the screen siren that he dropped buttered crumpets on the hotel's expensive carpets and then blurted out the fact that he was married. Dietrich, a traditionalist when it came to marriage, immediately changed her mind about an affair.

By the mid-Fifties, the asthma really began to take its toll on Donat, something that worried his legions of fans no end. He got hundreds of letters with suggestions on how to deal with it. One, quite bizarrely, advised him to kiss a goat, advice that he felt able to ignore! The reality was there was no cure and all he could do was to manage the condition and to take parts as and when his health allowed. In 1958 he played a Chinese mandarin alongside Ingrid Bergman in *Inn of the Sixth Happiness*, but it was clear to cast and crew alike that he was seriously ill. Donat took the old showbiz maxim 'the show must go on' seriously and he soldiered on bravely until the picture was completed. The day after filming ended he was rushed to hospital, where he died on 9 June 1958 at the age of fifty-three. Many thought he had succumbed to his asthma, or from complications linked to the condition, but it was discovered that he had a brain tumour the size of a very large egg. It made his struggle to finish the movie all the more heroic.

Robert Donat, the sickly lad from Withington, achieved greatness on a global scale thanks to his exploits in the film industry. Yet he would probably like to be remembered for his work in the theatre, which he refused to abandon despite the blandishments of Hollywood and the massive financial rewards on offer. That was the mark of the man.

4

THE WOOLWORTH'S FIRE

Woolworth's was long established in Manchester with its purpose-built premises dating from 1929. It was one of the most popular shops in the city centre, holding its own against close rivals Debenhams and the upmarket Kendal's on Deansgate. Selling everything from clothes and toys to records and electrical goods, Woolworth's Piccadilly had six floors and two basement areas, and was said to be the company's largest outlet in Europe, with around a hundred-and-fifty staff. 'Woolies' had always been the people's store and its cafeteria in particular proved a popular destination for elderly shoppers watching their pennies. Located on the second floor next to the furniture department it was busy throughout the day, serving breakfast, lunch and snacks.

On Tuesday, 8 May 1979, the doors opened at nine in the morning, just as they did every weekday. A few early shoppers trundled in, but there were no sales promotions and no reason to suggest that this would be anything other than a normal day. In fact, taking advantage of a quiet period the store was undergoing minor maintenance and the second-floor furniture department was being redecorated using paint-spraying equipment. The area had been cleared of stock and the display items stacked against a wall, ready to be returned to their normal place within forty-eight hours.

Business got brisk around lunchtime with perhaps five hundred people spread over the five floors, a high proportion of them, as per usual, in the cafeteria. By ten past one, painter John Lea had eaten his lunch and got stuck into his work again refurbishing the furniture department. He began spraying paint onto a wall when something glistened and caught his eye. Right away he knew there was a problem and he turned to where the furniture was stacked a few feet away.

Lea's instincts were spot on: flames were rising five feet in the air from behind wardrobes, chairs and beds. There was no smoke, only flames, indicating that the blaze had started quickly rather than having smouldered for a time. Lea raced down his ladder, shouting 'Fire!' at the top of his voice. He warned his colleague then raced into the nearby cafeteria where up to a hundred people were eating. Lea shouted above the general hum of idle chatter, warning people that there was a fire and that everyone had better get out quickly. He then went to look for the manager.

'It was strange,' the painter recounted later. 'People didn't seem to react or behave as though a fire had just started a few yards away. I shouted there was a fire again and this time they began to move out.'

Lea found store manager David Williams and moments later a fire bell began ringing. After trying unsuccessfully to locate a hose, Lea realised his pressurised paint-spraying equipment might explode so he returned to where he had been working to move his gear as far away from the fire as possible. The flames were now licking the ceiling and a thick blanket of smoke had begun edging towards the cafeteria.

Lea headed for the escalator and spotted a colleague coming up carrying a hose. The pair were keen to help but before they could begin dousing the flames they were met by store manager Williams, already suffering from the effects of inhaling thick black smoke, which by now was engulfing the whole floor. The manager's face was blackened and blood was seeping from a wound on his leg where he had kicked out a window to release smoke; clear evidence that remaining in the building was futile. The fire had spread at breakneck speed and anybody who came into contact with the smoke would have little chance of survival.

There was nothing John Lea or his colleague could possibly do except get out as quickly as possible. Lea turned and gave a rueful glance as he left but could see nothing other than a blanket of death. With a feeling of helplessness, he turned and made for the exit, reaching the safety of the street by twenty past one. Though it is hard to believe, records later suggested that the fire brigade would not be called for another nine minutes, by which time many people were already dead and the building well alight. There were even suggestions that the store's own switchboard had failed to make a call to the emergency services, with an operator claiming she had misheard a remark from a member of staff telling her there was a fire on the second floor: she thought her colleague had said there was a 'fight' on the second floor. With every second critical, who knows what might have happened had the call been made immediately?

Meanwhile, people were still trapped in the building and those on the second floor now had a matter of minutes before they too inhaled a toxic mixture of smoke and poisonous gasses. Some, like Stephanie Cassell, a 25-year-old Woolworth's cashier, broke windows and shouted down for help. She was one of the lucky ones because firemen were able to use crowbars and pickaxes to cut the metal bars on the windows while specialist cutting equipment was being prepared. Some customers, attempting to get out of the fire's path, went upstairs, several as far as the roof, to face what must have been a terrifying sight of flames and smoke billowing up from below.

Gerald Richardson, 67, a retired cosmetics rep, was working alone in the fourth-floor stockroom, when he noticed it was filling up with smoke. Terrified, he smashed a window and edged his way outside, perching precariously on a narrow ledge. Lucky for him he was spotted by firemen and was rescued, the last person in the building to be led to safety by the fire-fighters.

The fire brigade, now in attendance, battled valiantly to bring the blaze under control with some twenty-six engines camped around the gathering inferno and a hundred-and-fifty firemen either combating the fire or rescuing people from windows around the building. On two occasions fire-fighters had to be rescued after being trapped by the all-consuming conflagration. The whole scene was caught by television cameras and people at home looked on anxiously, praying that no one would succumb. Outside the store, thousands of people gathered in Piccadilly, watching in horror as fifteen-foot flames shot up the side of the building. By now screams could be heard, along with the sirens of ambulances ferrying the victims to hospital.

The third and fourth floors were by now raging out of control and the focus switched to saving those on the roof, whose number included a pregnant woman. Fortunately, it was a battle they would win. By four o'clock, the fire was extinguished and forty-seven people had been taken for medical treatment. Now came the grim task of finding bodies, an inevitability the emergency services accepted with a heavy heart as they began to search the charred remains of the cafeteria. Ten bodies were recovered, most close to the exit to the stairs: all had succumbed to toxic inhalation. In the cafeteria, remnants of half-eaten meals still lay on the tables. The timing of the blaze could not have been worse with lunch easily the busiest time of the day.

Shopper Joyce Carradous, was one of the first to have spotted the fire, as she later recounted.

> I saw flames perhaps seven feet high near some furniture. No-one else seemed to notice and I thought it might be some sort of advertising gimmick or even a demonstration for fire fighting.
>
> A young man who looked as though he might be staff passed by and I pointed it out to him and he rushed off. I decided to leave the store there and then and as I left the main entrance an alarm started to sound.

Joyce was one of the lucky ones, and in the days after the disaster stories of bravery, terrible coincidences and even stubbornness emerged from witnesses. Two of the victims, Hazel Heaton, 29, and her sister-in-law Susan Heaton, 28, a mother of two young children, had been on a lunchtime shopping trip to discuss Hazel's wedding plans. For whatever reason, they didn't make it out of the store alive. When later in the day Susan's 5-year-old son Paul returned from school alone, her husband Tom knew something terrible must have happened because Susan would never allow her son to be left on his own. Then a neighbour informed him that there had been a disaster in Manchester city centre. Tom's heart sank and he realised instantly that his children had lost their mother. 'I knew something awful must have happened,' he said. 'Then the police arrived.'

Cyril Baldwin had worked for four years at Woolworth's as a cleaner. His body was found beneath debris in the cafeteria and he would be the only member of staff to perish. The 68-year-old had been spotted at the top of an escalator, just seconds from safety, but had evidently turned back to try and save others. His widow, Betty, said it was typical of him not to run away from danger. 'He was a charismatic man who always did his best for his family and other people,' she said. Cyril's bravery cost him his life and he was not the only hero that day.

Helena Gunn, 69, had been expected home hours earlier, and a full line of dry washing in her garden was enough to cause concern for family and friends. Their suspicions weren't unfounded. Helena had been having lunch with lifelong friend Dorothy Botham in the cafeteria when news of the fire was first relayed. Undoubtedly, Helena had enough time to leave the area safely, but she would have had to have left her 86-year-old friend alone and facing certain death, something she couldn't contemplate. Dorothy had suffered a stroke the previous year and could walk only very slowly. With the majority of those in the cafeteria elderly, there was nobody to assist the two friends and their bodies were found with the others, just a few feet away from the safety of the stairs. Perhaps Cyril Baldwin had attempted to help them because he wouldn't have put his life in danger merely to stand and watch. Helena's son said at the time.

> My mother was very energetic but Mrs Botham was unsteady on her feet – she wouldn't have stood a chance in a fire that spread so quickly.
> I think my mother must have stayed with her rather than save her own life. I'm sure she would rather have done that rather than abandon her old friend.

The lonely life of Oliver Andrews, 32, also ended in the cafeteria. Though physically able to escape, did he too attempt to save others, paying the ultimate price? Mr Andrews lived in a nearby Salvation Army hostel and the manager of the hostel, Major Harding, said, 'He seemed a lonely man. We know of no next of kin to inform about his terrible death. All we know is that he came from Northern Ireland and may have had a sister living in Timperley.'

Pat Simmons had travelled into Manchester to meet her friend over lunch, but the friend could not make it and the 62-year-old spinster dined, and died, alone. That left the lady whom fate had conspired to save shattered: if death had a design for the Woolworth's fire, Pat was included, but her friend was not. For one elderly man who escaped the fire, his date with death was not cancelled. As he stumbled out onto the street, gasping for air but thankful of his narrow escape, a passing car knocked him down and he later died in hospital leaving his grief-stricken relatives unable to comprehend such wretched misfortune.

Perhaps the most unusual tale concerned Albert McNally. A spot of lunch at Woolworth's had become a central part of his daily routine and having bought his customary bowl of soup and settled at his favourite table, a collection of people burst in to warn the customers of the fire that was, by then, spreading rapidly. Time was of the essence, but not for Albert, who refused to leave until he had finished his meal.

Rebecca Kelly, who worked in the tea bar, rushed over to Albert when the alarm was raised and tried to get him to evacuate, but was left in disbelief as he insisted he was not going anywhere. 'I told him to leave by the nearest exit,' said Miss Kelly. 'He told me he had just got his soup and carried on eating. I said, "OK, it is you or your life," and he just grunted and kept on eating.' It was the last time Albert was seen alive, paying an extraordinary price for his last meal. He either didn't believe there was any serious danger, or didn't care. Other victims named were Sarah Bird, 68, Ernest Naylor, 73, and Michael Archer, 31, a homeless man whose identification proved the most difficult for forensic experts.

*

The inquest began four months later at Manchester town hall, with the main issue to be addressed the source of the fire. A spark from a plug socket behind the stored furniture was on the face of it a plausible explanation while one forensics expert took the view that a faulty electrical cable was the cause. Some of the fire officers believed a naked flame was to blame while reports of a fireball ripping through the second floor suggested possible terrorist activity, but this would eventually be ruled out by investigators mainly because no explosion was heard.

It was a frustrating process and that was reflected in the findings of the Manchester coroner, Leonard Gorodkin, who reached no firm conclusions as to the cause. In later years, a man claimed to have started the fire deliberately, but police were satisfied he was no more than a Walter Mitty character, desperately craving attention, and no charges were brought.

The decision to stack chairs and sofas against the wall of the furniture department was heavily criticised. One senior fire-prevention officer claimed that had the area been inspected on the day, the potential risk would have been spotted. Once alight, the stack of furniture produced a chimney effect, sending flames licking across the ceiling and igniting the deadly polyurethane fumes that had built up. The fire needed an air supply to intensify and a nearby escalator would have enabled it to spread quickly, with temperatures reaching eight hundred degrees at its outer edges. The very high concentrations of toxins meant anyone who breathed the lethal cocktail of smoke and gasses that preceded the fire had little chance of survival.

It emerged that sprinkler systems could well have averted the tragedy, but as they were not a legal requirement advice received from the fire authorities was ignored. It was noted that Marks and Spencer made sprinkler systems 'a matter of policy' and many criticised Woolworth's for opting for the cheapest available alternative. The reason was almost certainly cost; fitting sprinklers would have meant a 400 per cent increase in water rates. In fact, the new rates would have been £2,132 per year, a small price to pay when lives were at stake. Another problem the disaster brought to light was that the foam used in the chairs was not flame resistant, a flaw common to most furniture of the time.

What made the tragedy worse in the eyes of Mancunians was that this was the second fire to strike the city centre in little over two years. On 20 January 1977, just a hundred yards away from the Woolworth's store, seven young women working as punch-card operators lost their lives in a blaze when they were trapped during an evening shift at a Victorian office block on China Lane.

If there is a silver lining it is that the disaster led to a major shake-up in the law. Fire consultant Bob Graham was involved in the Woolworth's investigation and subsequently campaigned to change the hopelessly outdated fire regulations. Although it would take the government many years to act, eventually it did the right thing, as Graham observed.

That fire led to the requirements that came upon owners of stores to train their staff what to do in the event of fire. Sprinklers became a mandatory requirement in large retail stores and of course, the controls on the fillings of upholstery furniture were tightened. All of that came as a direct result of the Woolworths fire, so a great deal of good has come out of a very tragic event.

At nine o'clock on 24 April 1980, almost a year after the worst post-war fire the city had experienced, Woolworth's Piccadilly reopened its doors to customers after a renovation programme costing £1.8 million. A new restaurant had been built on the first floor while the second-floor cafeteria – dubbed the 'Oven of Death' – was now a storeroom. An integral component in the rebuilding process was state-of-the-art fire prevention, including a sprinkler system.

The newly refurbished store didn't last long. Shoppers never forgot the nightmarish events of 8 May 1979 and the Piccadilly branch closed for good in 1986. Perhaps the spectre of death still hung heavily over the ill-fated premises, although it has to be conceded that this was a period of general downsizing in the company's British operations.

More than three decades on the cause of the blaze remains unsolved. But today, shopping in major stores is immeasurably safer as a result of what happened in Manchester. Perhaps the relatives of those who perished can take some comfort from this.

5

THE PEOPLE'S PAINTER

They queued up from first light. They had travelled the length and breadth of Britain to see the work of a man they believed was one of the greatest artists this country has ever produced. Despite what snooty metropolitan critics might say, to the man in the street Laurence Stephen Lowry was a genius, someone from the humblest of backgrounds who had carved his name into the pantheon of artistic greats. He may have painted ordinary folk in ordinary surroundings but he did so with passion, with an obvious empathy for his subjects, and how the British public loved him for it. He was truly the people's painter.

It was September 1976. The venerable Royal Academy was mounting the biggest Lowry exhibition ever seen at its Burlington House headquarters in Mayfair, right in the heart of the capital's exclusive art world. There were more than four hundred paintings on display, ranging from classic industrial scenes to works we do not often associate with Lowry: sensitive portraits, stunning rural landscapes, elegant drawings of yachts. As soon as the show was announced the Academy knew it had a hit on its hands. The demand for tickets was overwhelming and by the time the exhibition closed ten weeks later no less than 350,000 people had attended. The Lowry had broken all known sales records. It was a quite remarkable result, given that the Royal Academy had been putting on exhibitions since its foundation in 1768. The only sour note was that the man himself had died just a few short months before opening day. He had not lived to see his greatest triumph.

As people waited patiently to go through the hallowed portals of

Burlington House, the GUS brass band (on three occasions, champions of the world) played a selection of tunes from their repertoire. There is no doubt that Lowry, a true Northerner, would have appreciated the choice of music. Suitably entertained the crowds poured into the gallery, at last able to appreciate the riches inside.

It was also evident that many in the tight circle of art critics and connoisseurs, who had not always been sympathetic to Lowry's work, were finally coming to appreciate what the public had known for years: that the man was a genius. The change in attitude had been a long time coming, and although the verdict was by no means unanimous, most of those who reviewed the exhibition recognised that the body of work he had built up over decades was exceptional. In her review for the *Sunday Times*, Marina Vaizey writes: 'This exhibition convinces me Lowry is a genius, and for two reasons. One is simply the technical base from which he worked; the innovatory skill of his techniques . . . the other is the tenacity with which he pursued his uncomfortable visions.' Noting the thousands who are flooding into Burlington House, Vaizey is surprised because his paintings are not, she notes, either quaint or picturesque. 'They attest to a brutal truth and yet we love them.' But she perhaps puts her finger on the reason for his popularity: 'Is this because he puts into images our internal feelings about life as it is lived? The crowded routine of work and play? Its aimlessness and inevitability?'

He painted 'life as it is lived'. Lowry would have settled for that.

By the 1970s, of course, Lowry had also been lauded by the artistic, academic and political elites. In 1962 he was elected to full membership of the Royal Academy, the most prestigious accolade of all for a British artist and one he was delighted to get because it had come from his peers. In 1965 he was given the freedom of the city of Salford and two years later the Post Office did him the great honour of issuing a stamp depicting one of his industrial scenes. He was awarded a clutch of honorary degrees, including a doctor of law from the University of Manchester and a doctor of letters from the University of Salford. Politicians rushed to honour him: in 1955, Prime Minister Harold Macmillan offered the OBE, while his Labour counterpart Harold Wilson tried to get him to accept both the CBE and a knighthood; he refused all three. Whether he rejected these offers out of genuine modesty, or because, as he told people, his mother was not around to see him fetching up at Buckingham Place, we shall never know.

In addition, during the last twenty years of his life, Lowry had become wealthy, so wealthy in fact that he was able to buy expensive paintings, most notably works from the Pre-Raphaelite school he so admired. After decades of struggle, both financial and artistic, he had reached the top of the pile. Given the circumstances in which he was brought up it was an unlikely rise.

Laurence Stephen Lowry was born on 1 November 1887 at 8 Barrett Street, Trafford, a modest semi-detached house. He was the only child of Robert and Elizabeth Lowry and was always known as Laurie by his parents. From the very moment he came into the world he disappointed his mother, who had been desperate for a daughter. It would not be the last time he let her down. His father's family was not in any way distinguished but his mother's had achieved a measure of success in business: her father, William Hobson, had run a successful hat shop in the city, enabling him to pay for the finer things in life for his daughter, including piano lessons and tickets for classical-music concerts. It was the type of genteel lifestyle she would yearn for after her marriage to Robert Lowry.

Elizabeth Lowry's main priority was to live in the most salubrious area in Manchester and when Laurie was aged ten she achieved her goal. They moved to Victoria Park, one of the wealthiest suburbs in the city and home to some of its most prominent citizens. It meant a huge increase in their rent and living costs and as if this was not enough the Lowrys took on a live-in housemaid. Given that her husband was a humble clerk with a firm of estate agents and property managers, and would never be granted the partnership he coveted, the financial burden was crippling. Robert Lowry said nothing, despite knowing full well they were living beyond their means. He, like his young son, was completely dominated by Elizabeth.

The strain on the family's finances became even more pronounced when Elizabeth decided to educate Laurie privately, at Grafton House School. It was money down the drain. He hated Grafton House and was teased mercilessly by pupils and masters alike for his solitary nature and his appearance. The latter caused particular amusement: he was very tall for his age and his flat feet meant the way he walked was very ungainly, with some comparing his gait to that of a puppet; to top it off he had a large head, which was permanently tilted, and a shock of unruly sandy hair. He did not fare any better academically, performing poorly in class and finding it difficult to finish his homework. It came as no surprise when he left school without passing a single exam. In short he was a misfit, with few prospects.

All of this came as a grievous disappointment to his mother, who expected him to go to university and thereafter to become a 'Manchester Man': hard-working, serious minded, respectable, successful in business. This was after all the world's first great industrial city, the legendary Cottonopolis, a place where anything was possible. Instead Laurie left school at fifteen and found a job as a clerk with Thomas Aldred and Son, chartered accountants, at 88 Mosley Street, where he would be employed for four years.

It was not the life he would have chosen for himself. He had always been keen on painting and drawing and in later life he would tell people that he had applied to Manchester School of Art. There is no proof that he made such an application and indeed he might, in the final analysis, have decided against it for fear of displeasing his mother. She took the view that art was all well and good as a hobby but not as a serious profession. Things did not look promising: stuck in a dead-end job, forced to endure a family life in which his mother tolerated no dissent, cut off from the one activity he enjoyed.

The young man desperately needed a break. Luckily, a saviour was at hand: his aunt, Mary. Seeing his obvious dissatisfaction with the job in Mosley Street, and his general unhappiness, she somehow persuaded Elizabeth, her sister, to let Laurie take evening classes with Reginald Barber, who lived in Fallowfield. More than anything, getting involved in art was a release from the mundane routine of clerical work and the domestic dominance of his mother. There was little else in life that he valued, as he later confessed: 'I went in for art as I was fit for nothing else. It was any port in a storm.'

After a spell with Barber he was accepted as a part-time student with Manchester School of Art in 1905. It was here that he met the figure who would be the greatest influence on his work: his teacher, Adolphe Valette.

'Mr Monsieur', as everyone called Valette, took the life class and was an artist of no mean ability; a man who had known the great Impressionists while working in Paris. He looked the part too, with his black beard, black hair and black cloak: if someone had made a doll depicting the typical French artist it would have looked like Mr Monsieur.

Valette brought a touch of Parisian glamour to Manchester: 'I cannot overestimate the effect on me at that time of the coming into this drab city of Adolphe Valette, full of the French Impressionists, aware of everything that was going on in Paris. He had a freshness and breadth of experience that exhilarated his students,' Lowry would later say. The two men, teacher and student, rubbed along well together and while his classmates at the school of art found Lowry something of an oddity, Valette never stopped encouraging him, despite harbouring doubts about his pupil's prospects of ever becoming a serious artist.

In fact it was an event outside the classroom that transformed his prospects. In 1909 the Lowry family moved from leafy Victoria Park to the much less salubrious suburb of Pendlebury in Salford. The move was a financial necessity and came about because his parents could no longer afford their current home. Although Elizabeth Lowry hated her new surroundings of mills, factories and cramped terraced houses, her husband's modest income left them with no option.

At first Laurie felt the same way as his mother did about Salford.

> In 1909 when I was twenty-two we moved from the residential side of Manchester to Pendlebury, which was a suburb of Salford and as industrial as it could be. At first I didn't like it at all. It took me six years. Then I got used to it; after that interested. I wanted to depict it. I couldn't recollect that anyone else had ever done it before. Finally, I became obsessed by it and I did nothing else for thirty years.

The story goes that his obsession with the industrial scenes came as a result of a divine revelation, or something close to it. Lowry would relate how one day he missed a train from Pendlebury and decided to continue his journey on foot. On his walk he looked up and saw the Acme Spinning Company's mill. As Lowry tells it he 'experienced an earthly equivalent of some transcendental revelation'. Whether it was such a dramatic transformation is open to doubt. What cannot be doubted is his commitment to depicting the industrial landscapes of Manchester and Salford, a commitment that was almost spiritual in its intensity.

He was no longer Laurie Lowry. It is not fanciful to suggest that he had become L. S. Lowry.

The fact that he had a withdrawn nature and a rather solitary existence helped his creative juices flow freely.

> Had I not been lonely none of my work would have happened. I should not have done what I've done, or seen the way I saw things. I work because there's nothing else to do. Painting is a marvellous way of passing the time and very interesting when you get into it.

His job was also a relevant factor. Made redundant in 1910 by Thomas Aldred and Son after four years he managed to secure new employment as a rent collector and clerk with the Pall Mall Property Company in Brown Street. It would be his place of work for the next forty-two years. Although he was in the office for part of the week, on most days his job took him all over greater Manchester. He covered Longsight, Old Trafford, Hulme, Broughton and Withington, enabling him to get to know the city and its people. The job suited him and not just because he was no longer tied to a desk. His new bosses had a relaxed, almost indulgent attitude towards their employees, taking the view that as long as the rent was collected in full and on time they could come and go more or less as they pleased. It suited Lowry down to the ground. On his rounds he had time to look and learn, to make sketches, to develop ideas for paintings that he could work on later at home. He built up an intimate knowledge of the city, its streets, its factories and mills; most of all, its people.

Despite the tuition from Valette and the opportunity to paint, the road to artistic success was a long, hard and rocky one. His unique style did not develop overnight. He worked on it, month after month, year after year. At first there was little encouragement from those around him; his mentor, Adolph Valette, was at best lukewarm while his mother, destructive as always, told him his pictures were ugly and pointless.

For years he despaired of seeing his work selling for more than a few pounds and he often lamented that the cost of brushes, paints and canvases meant that he was actually losing money from his art. In those dog days of the 1920s and 1930s, he would later say, 'nothing ever happened'.

It wasn't true that nothing ever happened. It would be more accurate to say that when something did happen it usually ended in disappointment. A good example is his first exhibition, which was held in Manchester in 1921, in the offices of a firm of architects, Rowland Thomasson, of 87 Mosley Street. While it received a glowing review in the *Manchester Guardian* – a newspaper that was always one of his greatest supporters – he failed to sell a single painting. It was the same story when his work went out to exhibitions up and down the country; they always came back unsold.

There was one occasion on which he did manage to sell a few pieces but even that was a disappointment. He was given a one-man exhibition in the spring of 1930. It was held in Manchester at the Round House, Every Street and featured twenty-five pencil drawings of Ancoats. At first glance it appeared to be successful as all twenty-five works were sold. The problem was, Lowry complained, that the prices were too low: at three guineas for an unframed drawing and four guineas framed he was hardly about to make a fortune, especially as expenses had to be deducted from the gross.

He would also have appreciated more support from Manchester. The city of his birth, he felt, did not rate him, a feeling that was confirmed by the prices paid by Manchester's municipal art galleries for two of his works: the oil painting, *An Accident*, and a drawing, *Stony Brow*. He was paid just £21 for the painting, which a couple of decades later would be valued in the tens of thousands, and even less for the drawing. It was perhaps understandable that he later told a friend 'they don't like me in Manchester'.

His failure to achieve success worth talking about must have been soul destroying, not to say humiliating. The fact that he carried on was due to his determination and strength of character. That and the support of a woman who would become the most influential person in his career after Valette. Her name was Daisy Jewell.

Miss Jewell was a senior executive with the firm of James Bourlet and Sons, a prestigious firm of art dealers based in London. She spent a lot of time in Manchester on business and it was on one of her trips north that, thanks to a mutual friend, she became acquainted with Lowry. From the first time she set eyes on his work, Daisy Jewell saw what no one else could: that this shy, self-effacing rent collector from Manchester could become a leading figure in the art world. With her undoubted charisma and contacts, she thought, his work could be brought to a mass audience.

It took time, a long time, sixteen years to be precise. She displayed his work in Bourlet's, sent it to exhibitions all over England and even to the fashionable salons of Paris. Despite her prodigious energy, progress was slow. There were the same familiar tales of his work failing to find a buyer and being shipped back to London. Then, in 1938, she made the breakthrough. Jewell heard that a director from the influential Lefevre Gallery was to call at Bourlet's. It was an opportunity she could not pass up.

The visitor's name was A. J. McNeill Reid, a highly influential figure in the fine-art scene. Art dealing was in Reid's genes. His father, Alexander Reid, from Glasgow, had been an artist himself but had turned his hand to buying and selling paintings, a field in which he had few peers. Reid senior had a keen eye for a painting and was perhaps the first to recognise the genius of a struggling artist from Holland who went by the name of Vincent Van Gogh. While they were living in Paris, Reid and Van Gogh shared an apartment for six months and the two grew close, with the Dutchman painting two portraits of the Scotsman, one of which he gave to him as a present. Alexander Reid did all he could to promote the work of his friend but it fell on deaf ears and it would be decades before the Dutchman's genius was recognised, by which time that troubled soul would be dead.

The father had recognised the genius of Vincent Van Gogh. Would the son do the same for Laurence Stephen Lowry? Could McNeill Reid persuade the art world of his value while Lowry was still alive, something that his father had failed to do in the case of Van Gogh? Daisy Jewell certainly hoped so.

The story goes that on the day Reid was due to call, Jewell left a few of Lowry's street scenes strategically propped up against her desk. When McNeill Reid passed her office – the door had deliberately been left ajar – he spotted Lowry's paintings and had what can only be described as a eureka moment. The dealer immediately asked for more of Lowry's work to be delivered to his gallery. He promised that if his business partner liked them he would put on a show. His partner did like them and a show was duly arranged.

The Lefevre exhibition was an undoubted success. Many of the critics invited to view it lauded his work, including those from the *Sunday Times* and the *Observer*. More than twenty pieces were sold including one that to Lowry's delight was acquired by the Tate Gallery. It was the start of a long and mutually beneficial relationship with the Lefevre, which staged many more Lowry shows. In the years to come his reputation soared and the price of his paintings rose commensurately. Royalty came to appreciate him: the Queen Mother bought one of his paintings from Lefevre, and, in 1952, he was honoured to be appointed as an official artist for the coronation of Queen Elizabeth II. America too opened its doors, with the Museum of Modern Art in New York purchasing one of his industrial scenes.

As the years passed his income from art shot up, making him annual profits of more than £50,000 by the early 1970s, huge for the time. With the newly acquired wealth he bought a house in Mottram-in-Longdendale, The Elms, in which he was able to display his collection of works by the great Pre-Raphaelite artists. There was also, at long last, recognition of his true worth by the city of his birth. While Salford, his adopted city, had always been supportive, buying up his work in considerable quantities, Manchester was less enthusiastic. That all changed in 1959 when Manchester city art gallery put on a full retrospective with more than a hundred of his best works on display. Manchester pushed the boat out for Lowry, not before time in the opinion of many. He was now a prophet in his own land.

If things turned out well in his professional life the same could not be said of his personal life. An only child, his relationship with his parents had always been problematic. He was never particularly close to his father, who died in 1932. It was an event that would change his life completely, and not just because of the substantial debts his father left behind him (which Laurie, ever the dutiful son, paid off). His mother was now aged 76 and she was a woman who had never kept good health. She also found widowhood hard to bear and remained more or less bedridden for the last seven years of her life. The only person she could turn to was Laurie.

So the burden of caring for Elizabeth fell on her son and although he was a conscientious carer it was far from easy. As well as the stress involved in looking after an elderly relative, which came on top of his job and painting in his spare time, his mother steadfastly refused to acknowledge his quite remarkable talents. Nor did the triumph that was the Lefevre exhibition make a difference. Her recognition of his worth would have meant the world to him, but, stubborn and selfish to the last, she refused to change her tune. Elizabeth Lowry died in 1939, just a few months after the Lefevre show. In spite of the way she had treated him he was shattered, near suicidal in fact. It would take him years to get over her passing, but, slowly and surely, he recovered.

Now in his early fifties, with no ties and a good income, it might have been time for personal happiness. Perhaps even for him to marry. But it never happened, nor was it ever likely to happen. From a young age his relationships with women had been almost completely dysfunctional. In fact he seemed to have little interest in either romantic or physical love, admitting openly in his twilight years that 'I've never had a girl'. There was a fellow student at college with whom he developed what might be best described as a platonic friendship. It was probably the closest he ever came to a genuine relationship, but as he later explained it just seemed to fizzle out.

> There was *one* girl: at art school. We met in life class for three years; and used the same railway station to go home. It went on like that. When the summer holidays came we'd say 'See you again in October.' I never thought of arranging to see her. And one October she wasn't there . . . and that was the end of that.

Many have speculated that he never married, or even had a serious girlfriend, because he valued solitude so much. Lowry put it down to his obsession with painting, taking the view that with his job and then painting into the wee small hours every night, 'I couldn't have gone on as I did and been fair to a wife'. Nor can we assume that he was simply being discreet about the women in his life. There is no record of him ever having an adult relationship with a member of the opposite sex.

That is not to say he did not have relationships, of a kind, with women. He did but they were unusual and involved young girls, girls who were always much younger than him. Lowry took them under his wing. They were protégées; he was their mentor, sometimes almost their guardian. There is no proof that anything sexual was involved, not least from the girls themselves. They were local lasses, sometimes the daughters of friends and acquaintances, often with a keen interest in art. On one occasion he asked a pal if he could take his 13-year-old daughter and her young friend to the pantomime. These were more innocent times and permission was granted, so off they went; an outing that was to develop into a close friendship between the middle-aged artist and the two teenagers. The girls would often call at his house, separately and un-chaperoned, for tea and advice on painting.

His closest and most-enduring friendship was with Carol Ann Lowry, who despite sharing a surname was not related. The friendship started in 1957 when Carol Ann, who lived in Heywood near Rochdale, decided that she wanted to study art and indeed to make it her career. Her mother suggested writing to the well-known artist, L. S. Lowry, who of course also lived in the north-west. At first Lowry failed to reply, filing away Carol Ann's letter with the heaps of correspondence he regularly received. Then one day, on a whim, he dug out the letter and jumped on a bus to Heywood. Strange as it may sound the 70-year-old artist and the 13-year-old schoolgirl hit it off immediately.

He took her on outings; to the theatre, the ballet, for meals in Manchester city centre, trips that did not involve her parents, who were quite happy with their daughter's somewhat unusual friendship. The elderly artist and the schoolgirl would talk for hours on end about art, literature, her father's job in a mill; the age gap mattered little to either of them. As the years passed Lowry supported her financially, paying the fees at the convent school she attended and for Saturday-morning art classes at Rochdale College of Art. They would go on holiday together, just the two of them, but there was never anything untoward about their relationship, as Carol Ann confirms.

> Very much later, when I was grown up, people put it into my head
> that he might have felt differently towards me, as a man feels towards a

woman, but I absolutely cannot believe it to have been so. I don't think there was ever a physical thing for him, with any woman.

It suited both parties. He was looking for someone to care for, perhaps to compensate for the family he never had, while she had found a 'fairy godfather who came along with gifts, not merely material gifts, but gifts of character and education'. He supported her when she attended an art college in Swansea and at graduation time he bestowed a five-figure sum on her. Carol Ann later got a teaching job on the Isle of Wight, where she married a local man, but she never lost touch and she and husband John would often travel north to visit Lowry.

Despite being so close, Carol Ann got the shock of her life when Lowry died in 1976. It was not just the normal feelings we all have at the passing of someone we have become attached to. Rather it was the contents of his will. He had left her nearly £300,000, a huge sum for the time, plus a selection of his paintings and drawings, themselves worth a great deal of money. He had never mentioned the legacy, joking to her that she would get a piano and a sideboard when the day came.

There was another shock. Many of the drawings he bequeathed to her portrayed girls in a variety of bizarre, and very tight, costumes. It is as if the girls had been forced into the clothes and while the works are not pornographic they have a definite erotic edge. Many experts felt that the eroticism portrayed in them reveals a darker side to Lowry.

In conclusion let us turn from Lowry's personal life and consider his place in art history, a subject that would have been of much more importance to him. Despite his massive popularity with the public he has been consistently scorned by a small yet significant number of commentators. Those who do not rate him speak disparagingly of his 'matchstick' men and the primitive qualities of his industrial scenes. His fiercest critic is undoubtedly the snooty, London-based critic Brian Sewell, who described Lowry as a 'nincompoop' whose 'ponderously booted matchstick men, urban idiots and pop-eyed portraits are the work of a trivial painter, a man of tricks, mannerisms and small things'. Others have been less harsh, but remain unimpressed. William Feaver, art critic of the *Observer*, argued that Lowry was happy to stay in his comfort zone: 'In all those years his preoccupations hardly changed.'

Then, in 1976, when Lowry died, and it was revealed to the world that he had worked for decades as a rent collector, there were howls of derision in many quarters. How could a man from Salford, the industrial north of England, a man with little formal education, a part-time painter, be considered a serious artist they asked?

That condescending attitude has largely been swept away in recent years. The building of the splendid Lowry Gallery in Salford Quays in the late 1990s is a fitting tribute from the city where he lived and worked and, more importantly, having a space dedicated to his work has added greatly to his lustre. A 2011 documentary, *Looking for Lowry*, also did much to enhance his reputation. In the film Sir Ian McKellen, the great Shakespearean actor, and a Northerner (he was raised in Wigan), insists that Lowry has been shamefully neglected by the art establishment in general and the Tate Gallery in particular. Given the Tate's primary purpose is to showcase British art that, he says, is unforgiveable.

The Tate to its credit listened and in June 2013 Lowry was given a major exhibition, the first of its kind by a public institution since his death. It also featured paintings by the French Impressionists in order that their style and vision could be compared with Lowry's. As the organisers noted his work is in that great artistic tradition initiated by the likes of Monet and Renoir, distinguished company indeed.

Serious art dealers and collectors no longer have any doubt about Lowry's worth. These hard-headed businessmen who regularly gather at Sotheby's and Christie's back their judgments with hard cash and recently they have piled into Lowrys with bucket-loads of it. In 2011 his *Piccadilly Circus* was sold at Christie's for £5.6 million, matching the world record set by another of his paintings, *The Football Match*. Observing that the fourteen Lowrys in the Christie's sale had realised a staggering £17.6 million, the head auctioneer made the point that the market for his work had never been stronger.

It seems that at long last public, critical and commercial tastes have converged. The days of Lowry being patronised and ignored have long gone.

He deserves nothing less.

6
THE BEAST OF MANCHESTER

Trevor Hardy was in trouble with the authorities for most of his life and the seriousness of his crimes escalated steadily: from childhood misdemeanours, to burglary and on to vicious assaults, before, almost inevitably, he started to kill. So horrific were the crimes that even experienced police officers were left sickened by the work of the man the press were to dub 'The Beast of Manchester'. His murder spree lasted for fifteen months, from New Year's Eve 1974 until March 1976 and while he roamed the streets, no woman was safe.

Hardy was anything but a model pupil. Desperately unpopular at school, he bullied classmates and intimidated teachers and, on one occasion, there was a frightening glimpse of his explosive rage and utter contempt for women. After being sent out of a lesson he had disrupted, Hardy went into the school hall and proceeded to perform a series of somersaults and handstands. A female teacher caught him and slapped him across the face. In an instant, Hardy tried to grab her around the throat but she managed to wriggle free, only for him to attempt to batter down a door she had escaped through. A fellow pupil recalled, 'Everyone was frightened of him. He was a nasty boy who became an evil man and his mere presence was enough to put people on edge.'

Hardy continued to cause mayhem throughout his teens, which would see lengthy spells in approved schools, borstal and remand homes before judges tired of his antics and sent him to prison aged only fifteen. Well-meaning attempts to show him a different path were futile; he was a ticking time-bomb whose behaviour became increasingly erratic and violent. He found it difficult to hold down a job and more often than not he would take on labouring jobs and work on demolition sites, living in a succession of council flats in Failsworth.

In his private life he found it hard to maintain relationships. He was a transvestite and wore his mother's clothes and make-up, and his social life involved making friends with local schoolchildren who were playing truant. Despite most of the youngsters being half his age, he invited them into his home and supplied them with food, cigarettes and alcohol, adopting the role of 'gang leader'. Emotionally, he was immature and he would fly into blind rages, hitting the children before apologising profusely. Worryingly, one girl was of particular interest to him and he engineered situations at his home that would invariably lead him to be alone with her.

When they first became acquainted, Beverley Driver was the 10-year-old daughter of a friend and despite the fact that she had always known Hardy as 'Uncle Trev', he fantasised about having a physical relationship with her. Hardy clearly believed the girl was more than just a friend and despite being given no more encouragement than the odd peck on the cheek, he became obsessed, believing she was his. Her family, concerned about the amount of time their daughter was spending in his company, wanted her to end all contact with him. Wary of his terrible temper, however, they knew the time would have to be right for her to end the association.

In 1971, she was given the perfect opportunity finally to rid herself of Hardy when he was arrested for a serious assault that could just as easily have ended in murder. When out on a heavy drinking session one evening, Hardy accused Stanley O'Brien of failing to buy a round of drinks and exacted revenge by attacking him from behind with a pickaxe. O'Brien survived the assault leading Hardy to express disappointment that he had not struck his victim harder.

By now aged twenty-seven, he was given a five-year prison sentence for the assault and it was while serving time that he received news that would finally turn him from a violent bully into a psychopath. While the now 14-year-old Beverley Driver was writing Hardy a letter saying how much his 'gang' of teenagers was missing him, her father happened to glance over her shoulder. Disturbed by what he read, he demanded she throw the letter away and write a different one, effectively ending the relationship with Hardy. Little could Beverley have realised the revised letter would start a chain reaction that would cost three women their lives.

Hardy's reaction was that of a spurned lover, weeping as he read the letter before becoming incandescent with rage. He finally came to the conclusion that he would kill Beverley upon his release, and planned a grisly end for her, while also plotting to finish off the hapless Stanley O'Brien, whom he blamed for the loss of Beverley. For three years and two months he was kept going by pure hatred and a determination to punish those he saw as his tormentors. The only thing keeping both Driver and O'Brien alive was Hardy's incarceration, although as the days and weeks passed, their time was running out.

In November 1974, his murderous instincts were helped by a decision that defies belief: he was granted parole for good behaviour inside. This was despite being only halfway through his sentence and having a string of convictions stretching back more than two decades. The authorities had let a monster loose on an unsuspecting Manchester.

Whether he knew, and died of fear, Stanley O'Brien passed away due to natural causes just days before Hardy was released, meaning that Beverley Driver was now the sole focus for Hardy's depraved thoughts. He wasn't about to rush things. Cold and calculating, he wanted to savour his act of vengeance and planned first to terrorise his victim and her family through a series of gruesome threats. Driver, now seventeen and a newlywed, was oblivious to the danger she faced. Happy to be married she had forgotten about Hardy and assumed he had done the same. She couldn't have been more wrong and when a local girl went missing, Beverley had no idea that Hardy had begun his reign of terror.

The senseless killing of 15-year-old Janet Lesley Stewart is one of the most chilling examples of being in the wrong place at the wrong time. It was on the night of New Year's Eve 1974 when Hardy's obsession finally turned to murder. Half-drunk, consumed with hatred and looking for trouble, he was walking near playing fields on Ten Acres Lane, Newton Heath around eleven o'clock. When a car pulled up a little way ahead of him a girl got out and a voice shouted, 'see you tomorrow, Les'. The car then drove off.

However, to Hardy, those words sounded like, 'see you tomorrow,

Bev'. The girl was the same age and build as Beverley Driver. 'It must be her,' he thought. He couldn't believe his luck. He had imagined this moment over and over again for almost four years. Hardy followed her across the darkened fields and when she turned to see who was behind her, she saw a balding man of twenty-nine with death in his eyes.

'What do you want?' she trembled.

'Remember me, Bev?' he asked.

Of course, she didn't remember him because she had never set eyes on him. The dim orange lights from the nearby street meant that Hardy could barely see the girl's face. Another distinct possibility is that he just didn't care who it was: the pretty young teenager represented all the Beverley Drivers in the world. In an instant, he stabbed Janet in the throat and she died within seconds. Hardy then attempted to bury the body in a hollow before calmly walking home to watch a Hogmanay television show with his mother. When she was asleep, he crept out and buried the body in a nearby clay pit, a process that involved dismemberment and decapitation. Janet Stewart's family were left with a dread of what might have happened but a glimmer of hope for almost two years. Her corpse would lie undiscovered for twenty agonising months.

When Hardy read newspaper reports of a missing girl, last seen on playing fields on Ten Acres Lane, he realised his victim was not Beverley Driver. That meant he still had unfinished business and so he stepped up his campaign of terror by approaching local youths to help him find Beverley, who was now heavily pregnant. They passed on his message that Hardy 'was going to get her' and one youngster told her Hardy was going to 'chop her legs off with an axe'. Nobody knew he had already killed and so his threats were largely ignored, but he persisted and began to ratchet up his cowardly campaign.

A few months later, Hardy met Beverley's brother, Geoffrey, in the street and told him, 'she's as good as dead,' before taking out an axe from beneath his coat. He then chased the teenager home, where his increasingly concerned family considered their options. Later that night, an axe smashed through Beverley's bedroom window. Despite calls to the police for protection, Hardy was relentless in his pursuit.

After Beverley gave birth to a daughter, she returned home with her baby for what should have been the happiest time of her life. Then, out of the blue, there was a violent hammering on the Drivers' front door. It was Hardy, claiming he wanted to apologise for the axe incident. Disturbingly, he asked to see the infant at which point the child's father instinctively ran over to the pram to shield the baby from Hardy's view. Yet Beverley's father said it would be okay if Hardy was allowed a quick peek, perhaps believing it would calm him down. He bent over, smiled and gave an odd laugh, then turned to Beverley, handing her a pound note for a christening present before leaving. Only Hardy will know what was going through his mind but it's safe to assume it was no longer just Beverley Driver whose life was at risk.

Hardy's bloodlust, meanwhile, continued unabated and six months after his first murder, he struck again. Wanda Skala was an 18-year-old barmaid who worked in the Lightbowne hotel in Moston. In an incredible coincidence barman Bill Stewart, the father of Hardy's first victim Janet, whose remains lay undiscovered in a shallow grave, also worked in the Lightbowne. It's entirely possible that Mr Stewart, who didn't know for certain if his missing daughter was dead, served drinks to Hardy, her killer. Hours later, on a warm summer's night in July 1975, the horrific memories of New Year's Eve would come flooding back.

Hardy and his lover Sheilagh Farrow had been drinking for most of the evening and when Hardy told Farrow he was 'going to do a job', she assumed he was going to break into a house. She got on the night bus and left Hardy to get on with his 'work'. But burglary was the last thing on his mind.

As pretty Wanda Skala made her way home towards Luke's Walk, Hardy approached her, apparently with the intention of mugging the slightly built teenager. Wanda screamed and several residents heard the commotion, one woman peering out of her curtains as Hardy dragged the girl down an alley. After a brief struggle, he struck in the face with a brick before carrying her behind hoardings at the back of some houses. He took her handbag and fled, but, fearing she could identify him, he soon returned. Suffering terrible facial injuries, Wanda had managed to stand against a wall only to see Hardy standing a few feet away. He strangled her and savagely beat her with a large rock, biting off a nipple and repeatedly kicking her in the genitals.

No human being, let alone a young, innocent girl, deserves to die in such horrific circumstances and when Wanda's body was discovered the next day, even seasoned detectives were sickened by the ferocity of the attack. He would later claim the wounds he inflicted were merely to throw police off the scent but it's likely that the despicable acts he performed on the bodies of his victims were entirely for his gratification.

There were few real clues to the killer's identity. Forensic science in the 1970s was, to say the least, unsophisticated. Wanda's body would undoubtedly have had enough damning evidence on it immediately to convict the murderer if modern methods had been available. Hardy, however, had been at the pub and therefore fell under suspicion, but his girlfriend provided him with a cast-iron alibi, claiming that Hardy had been in bed with her all night and, being a light sleeper, she would have known if he had left the house. Farrow was either terrified or incredibly callous, as Hardy had already confessed the killing of Wanda Skala to her. She even wore the engagement ring of Janet Lesley Stewart on her finger.

It seems Hardy couldn't contain the fact that he was still at large after two seemingly random killings and while out for a drink with younger brother Colin, who had also been questioned about the killing of Wanda Skala, he admitted his guilt. Colin tried to prise more information out of his sibling, provoking him by saying he was making it up. The truth was he knew his brother was more than capable of murder and believed every word he was saying. Perhaps suspicious of the questioning from his younger brother, he became agitated and when they returned to Colin's flat, Hardy savagely beat him to within an inch of his life, warning Colin's wife not to call an ambulance. He left but returned minutes later to make beans on toast while his brother lay unconscious on the stairs.

Colin Hardy recovered from his beating and after discussing the situation with his wife, he decided there was only one course of action open to him. He told the police about his brother's confession. Hardy was arrested in October 1975 and detectives grilled him for three days. Fearing his teeth might match wounds left on the body, he had a file smuggled into his cell so he could grind his teeth down and frustrate possible attempts to link him with the crime. However, despite their strong suspicions, the police had to release him due to lack of evidence and a watertight alibi.

In a bizarre twist, just three months after being questioned about

Wanda Skala, Hardy was hailed as a hero as he tried to rescue a couple living above his flat on Smedley Road, Collyhurst during a house fire. Hardy scaled a drainpipe and attempted to rescue the pair from the roof before being beaten back by flames, leaving the fire brigade to save Graham and Christine Lovell. Hardy would later admit to starting the fire deliberately in the hope of being awarded a council house. Reports of the blaze and attempted rescue by Hardy appeared in the same edition of the *Manchester Evening News* that carried the story of the continuing search for Wanda Skala's killer.

It was several months before Hardy again lost control. In March 1976, he attacked a woman in the ladies toilet of the King's Arms in Hollinwood after claiming he had caught her in a 'lesbian embrace' with his girlfriend. He gripped her throat so tightly that she bit off part of her tongue, although she at least lived to tell the tale.

Fearing arrest, Hardy went on the run, living rough in derelict houses in the Failsworth area of Manchester or on canal banks, sleeping where and when he could, using the cover of darkness to commit petty crimes. With Sheilagh Farrow bringing him food and clothes he could have continued his reign of terror for some time, but, during a bungled robbery, he killed again.

The date was 9 March 1976 and as he attempted a break-in at Marlborough Mill in Failsworth, Sharon Mosoph, aged seventeen and returning from a party with workmates, disturbed him. Rather than be identified and captured, he strangled her, then stabbed her with a screwdriver before carrying out a series of mutilations. He dumped her naked body in the Rochdale canal, just three hundred yards from her home on Brookes Drive but then jumped into the freezing water in order to eradicate any damning teeth marks. Sharon Mosoph was discovered floating face down in the canal the following morning and was identified by her parents not long after.

Detectives believed they knew who the killer was and were now desperate to trace Trevor Hardy, who was still chief suspect in the murder of Wanda Skala. Hardy – possibly believing by this point he was above the law and certainly far cleverer than those who sought to stop his reign of terror – fled only a few miles to Stockport where he was tracked down. Of course, he had another alibi with the ever-willing

Farrow claiming she had been with him on the night of the murder. This time, however, his luck had run out. He was arrested and charged with the murder of both Wanda Skala and Sharon Mosoph.

While in custody at Strangeways, Hardy decided to confess to the murders he was suspected of to detective chief inspector John Bennion, as well as leading the police to the grave of Janet Stewart. In a forty-page statement detectives described as a 'dossier of death', Hardy admitted numerous other misdemeanours and also gave detailed accounts of the three murders, complete with maps.

Bennion said of Hardy, 'He's one of the strangest, coldest men I've ever met. Physically, he's like a whippet – small, but tremendously tough. And completely unemotional. He's never shown any remorse or emotion. No one really knows him. Why did he kill like this? There was no real reason.'

Yet again, he needed to take centre stage and at his trial, almost a year after his arrest, he elected to defend himself. In emotional scenes at Manchester Crown Court, an attempt was made by members of the murdered girls' family to attack him, requiring extra security to be drafted in. Hardy attempted a plea of manslaughter due to diminished responsibility, but one psychiatrist took the view that 'evil can't be disguised as illness,' while another expert claimed that Hardy was 'a very dangerous psychopath who could kill again at any time for many years'.

The plea was rejected by the court and on 2 May 1977, Trevor Joseph Hardy was found guilty of brutally ending the lives of three young women who had everything to live for. Jailed for life, the police suspected he may well have killed others, but were satisfied with the convictions. The families of the murdered girls later launched a campaign to put Sheilagh Farrow behind bars, too, but it seems she cut a deal with the authorities.

The father of Sharon Mosoph, Ralph, campaigned for Hardy to die in prison and demanded the Home Office reveal whether he was on a list of prisoners who would never be allowed to walk the streets. In June 1997 he got his wish when it was confirmed that in Hardy's case life would mean life. At the time, Mr Mosoph said, 'I feel like I've won the lottery. I'm just so happy.' It was a small victory considering his loss.

Trevor Hardy died following a heart attack in Wakefield prison on

25 September 2012. When they heard the news the Mosophs threw a party, with patriarch Ralph declaring, 'Me and my family think this is the best thing that's ever happened to us. It's like winning the lottery. We feel as though a burden has been lifted from our shoulders, knowing that he cannot come out and do anything to anybody else.'

7

THE MANCHESTER SOUND

The term Beatlemania has entered the *Oxford English Dictionary*. Its definition: 'extreme enthusiasm for the Beatles pop group, as manifested in the frenzied behaviour of their fans in the 1960s'. But the world is less aware of the huge impact Manchester bands made both in Britain and Stateside during the Swinging Sixties and especially during the golden year of 1965. It is a fact – albeit a lesser known one – that in the spring of that year groups from Manchester filled the number one, two and three spots in the American charts. And, for good measure, one of those bands would outsell the Beatles at a time when the Fab Four were supposedly at the peak of their popularity.

It was 8 April 1965 and when the United States hit parade was announced the *Manchester Evening Chronicle* excitedly announced to its readers that Manchester 'was poised to take over as the world's leading beat city,' outstripping Liverpool. This was no idle boast and the *Chronicle* went on to list the top three US singles:

1. 'I'm Telling You Now' Freddie and the Dreamers
2. 'Can't You Hear My Heartbeat?' Herman's Hermits
3. 'Game of Love' Wayne Fontana and the Mindbenders

For Freddie Garrity, who, with his Dreamers, had reached the pinnacle of the cutthroat and ultra-competitive music industry it was seventh heaven. 'I'm just knocked out. No words can describe how I feel,' he told one journalist. It was also good news for showbiz agent Danny Betesi of Kennedy Street Enterprises in Manchester, who represented all three groups.

The trio of Manchester bands were part of a British invasion of America. Astonishingly, no less than thirty of the top one hundred records on the US charts were by acts from the UK. The main industry paper, the legendary *Melody Maker*, noted the trend: 'Britain's pop blitz on America has reached amazing proportions. English stars like Freddie and the Dreamers, Herman's Hermits and Petula Clark are saturation-bombing America's charts with direct hits.'

It seemed that where the States was concerned, British acts were pushing at an open door, as Freddie Garrity explained: 'I think Britain is producing much better records than America now . . . even the Beach Boys have an English sound.' To be fair, he gave the Beatles tremendous credit for blazing the trail: 'The Beatles obviously opened things up twelve months back and everybody else pushed in right away. Our records were released in America before but they didn't seem to go and we felt a bit out of it.'

Peter Noone (aka 'Herman' of Herman and the Hermits) agreed with Freddie about the importance of the Fab Four in starting the craze for all things British: 'It's all due to the Beatles, the Beatles started everything. They want anything that's British now – clothes, shoes and hats. When I was last in America, we used to walk about Los Angeles and kids would stop us and wanted to buy our British clothes off us in the street!'

The Beatles' influence undoubtedly helped others from this side of the Atlantic to break the States. But why Freddie and the Dreamers and why Herman's Hermits, the two bands that made the biggest impact?

It is a question that is especially relevant in the case of Freddie Garrity, who was not blessed with either great musical ability or natural good looks. Freddie and the Dreamers got to the top thanks to sheer hard work, brilliant marketing and, it must be acknowledged, a generous dollop of good luck along the way.

Freddie Garrity was born in Manchester, the son of a miner, in 1936 (for publicity purposes, he always claimed to have come into the world four years later, in 1940) and attended Yew Tree secondary school in Wythenshawe. On leaving at the age of sixteen, he became an apprent-ice engineer, before working as a brush salesman and then taking up various sales-assistant positions in a variety of high-street stores.

But music was his passion (along with Manchester United) and in the first year of his apprenticeship he won a talent contest with an impression of Al Jolson. That encouraged his ambitions and with his brother Derek he performed in a group called the Red Sox, who would be runners-up in a local skiffle competition. He followed that with a spell in the John Norman Four but within weeks he left them to join the Kingfishers, the group that by 1961 would become Freddie and the Dreamers, although its original name was the Dreamers Rhythm Band. Most definitely the leader, Freddie was backed by Derek Quinn (lead guitar and harmonica), Roy Crewdson (rhythm guitar and keyboards), Pete Birrell (bass) and Bernie Dwyer (drums).

He worked hard to get bookings for his fledgling group, which was not appreciated by one employer: after failing to turn up for work this day, he was sacked by gents outfitter John Collier; in fact, he had been down in London to looking for gigs. Clearly, Freddie needed a job that would dovetail with his music and he came up with what he thought was the perfect solution. But it didn't work out that way.

> Eventually, I thought, I'll be a milkman. I can get up early, dash round with the milk and be finished by nine o'clock, so I can be song-writing and rehearsing for the rest of the day. I forgot that I'd be coming off stage later and so, when I overslept one weekend, I got sacked. That's when I turned professional.

Freddie and the Dreamers were neither the most talented musicians in the world, nor were they great singers. If they were going to get to the top they needed something that would make them stand out from the hundreds of other wannabe bands trying to make the big time. An X Factor if you like.

They found one. Freddie's zany personality.

As a performer he was irrepressible. One critic summed him up perfectly: 'Garrity was a clown who cavorted on stage like a demented marionette in a series of exaggerated dance steps . . . . He leapt, lunged and larked through every show.' Even his geeky looks and thick, horn-rimmed glasses proved advantageous; wrong for a heartthrob, perfect for the clown prince. While other bands relied on their sex appeal, the Dreamers used humour and natural energy. The highlight was Freddie's characteristic high jump, which took him several feet into the air, with his legs folded beneath him. They had honed the moves in their live performances, notably in Germany, where, like the Beatles, they had a residency in a nightclub.

Another routine developed out of a gig at Stockport County's stadium. Someone put a pair of shorts on the double bass, which encouraged them to start singing 'Short Shorts'. It was the first time he dropped his trousers on stage and although the routine became popular with the public, Garrity came to regret going down that particular road. 'I'm sorry now because I'm stuck with it. Everywhere I go people expect me to pull my trousers down.'

The comedy elements of the act covered a multitude of musical sins but it was especially suited to television, an increasingly important medium for the music industry. After his first appearance, on ITV, Freddie freely admitted the impact that his cavorting around the stage had made on the audience.

> We were seen on TV for the first time on *Thank Your Lucky Stars* and I came running down some steps, swinging my arms from right to left. It [their first hit 'If You Gotta Make a Fool of Somebody'] leapt up the charts after that. Let's face it the dance routines made our records as our sound was thin and weedy.

Lead guitarist Derek Quinn agreed, but believed that the emphasis on fooling around may not have been a good career move in the long run.

> Musically, we weren't that good. We thought that, if we did daft things, it would stop people noticing our faults. People came to see us because Freddie would leap all over the place. We actually got worse rather than better because we concentrated too much on dance routines.

Despite Quinn's misgivings the novelty aspects of the act did their careers no harm at all. In fact, they prospered, winning a recording contract with EMI. Shortly after, their version of 'If You Gotta Make a Fool of Somebody' reached number three in the British charts while the follow-up disc – 'I'm Telling You Now', co-written by Garrity – made it to number two.

By this time the band was mixing with the pop elite. There was a

UK tour with the Rolling Stones, on which the Dreamers topped the bill. And when the 'Big O', Roy Orbison, arrived in this country Freddie and the boys were on the bill. In fact, Garrity and Orbison became good friends, although they had to navigate through a very tricky social situation, as the Mancunian later explained.

> I had a house in Manchester, a two-up, two-down with an outside toilet, which cost me £600. I'd also bought an E-Type which was three times the price of the house. I wanted Roy to come for a meal before the show. He had a ranch with acres of land and here was me taking him to Coronation Street. I served him salad because I didn't know how to cook, and actually I'm embarrassed when I think about it.

Nevertheless, this was a golden age for Freddie Garrity and his band. There was more chart success: their Christmas release in 1963 was 'You Were Made for Me', which climbed to number two, selling more than three-quarters of a million copies. Described as nursery-rhyme pop, it wasn't to everyone's taste; on the popular BBC television show *Juke Box Jury*, Cilla Black said that it sounded like Freda and The Dreamers. The group's ability to clown and do slapstick made them ideal for other branches of showbiz. They made a first appearance in panto in 1963, starring in *Cinderella* at the Royalty Theatre, Chester and there were also film roles in *What a Crazy World* with Joe Brown and Marty Wilde.

By 1965, however, their star had begun to wane. There were still hits, but the discs did not sell in the same prodigious quantities as before. Fortunately, a much bigger prize came over the horizon: the good old US of A.

After releasing the single 'I'm Telling You Now', the group and its managers looked for a way to promote it, something memorable that would tie in with a three-minute single. After much deliberation they came up with a little dance routine, which they christened 'The Freddie'. Although Garrity would later claim it was devised 'for a laugh', 'The Freddie' caught on in spectacular fashion, especially in the States. No doubt due to demand from its readers, the *Manchester Evening Chronicle* published a handy guide to the new craze.

> Hop from left foot to right foot, throwing your arms out wide at each pivot in a way you might embrace a long-lost brother (or pop star).

Do this about half-a-dozen times or more, keeping in time with the music before switching to the bowing sequence. This is done by bending low and thrusting forward . . . . Follow up the bowing with the third basic movement – a couple of those mid-air leaps which are a high spot of Freddie's clowning. (8 April 1965)

Freddie himself came up with much more succinct instructions for the eponymous dance: 'It's rather like a farmer plodding his way through a muddy field, only more exaggerated.'

Although he would later dismiss 'The Freddie' as something they did for a laugh it turned out to be one of the shrewdest examples of marketing in pop history. America just couldn't get enough of 'The Freddie' and it became the number one teenage craze from New York to LA. Chubby Checker, the legendary rock-and-roll singer, even released a tribute single called 'Do the Freddie'. The lyrics below show that it wasn't the most sophisticated song ever recorded, but it raced up the charts nevertheless:

Are you ready?
Let's do The Freddie!
Move your hands to the sky
Kick your legs out high

Meanwhile the invitations for the five Mancunians to appear on top variety shows poured in, including one from Ed Sullivan, the biggest name on television. The Dreamers accepted them all, performing 'The Freddie' with gusto, and endearing themselves to the huge American audiences.

The effect of these appearances was immediate. Record sales were spectacular, and it was all down to their infectious personalities and the dance moves, as Freddie explained: 'Just like at home the visual approach sold us.' The single 'You Were Made for Me' shot to number one in the States, shifting more than a million copies in the process and earning the boys a gold disc, while their album, *Mercury*, sold by the barrow-load. As Freddie fever grew, thousands turned up for their live performances. In Syracuse, New York the police had to stop the concert three times as over-excited fans crashed through safety barriers, before using water cannon and calling in the riot squad. It was the same story in New Jersey – where four thousand fans tried to storm the stage, with order only being restored when the police brought in reinforcements – and in other states across America.

The commercial success of Freddie and the Dreamers made Garrity a wealthy man. By the mid-1960s he was living in a £9,000 luxury bungalow in Nansen Road, Gatley (houses there now sell for upwards of £500,000) with his wife, child and the family's two Pyrenean mountain dogs. He would later move south, to Dorset, becoming the proud owner of an eight-bedroom mansion complete with swimming pool and a garage big enough for his collection of sports cars. We can only assume that he would have been quite happy to invite the Big O to his little place in the country!

Despite the apparent domestic bliss, he was not averse to one of the perks on offer to the touring pop star: groupies. He found them hard to resist but as the saying goes, 'what happens on the road stays on the road'. Freddie agreed, explaining that 'I suppose I thought I could do anything I liked, so long as I didn't take it home with me.'

Inevitably, the hits did not last forever. By the late Sixties a new, harder edged, album-based music had emerged, epitomised by newcomers like The Doors and Jimi Hendrix and by established groups like The Beatles, who were able to adapt to the new sound. There was no place for the sweet and innocent songs of outfits like Freddie and the Dreamers. By 1971 the band had broken up, with Garrity embarking on a solo career. He reformed the Dreamers, with new personnel, in the mid 1970s and went back on the road.

Along the way this consummate entertainer also found time to appear on television, in both presenting and acting capacities. He was a drug-dealing disc-jockey in the popular ITV drama *Heartbeat* and also presented *Little Big Time*, a children's programme. There were hard times too. His voice started to go, forcing him to rely on a pre-recorded voice track, something that drew heavy criticism from the tabloid press. His private life was far from stable: in 1975, his first marriage, to Josie, ended in divorce, as did his second, to Dee. Marriage number three – to Chris, nineteen years his junior – followed in the early 1990s.

The touring continued until 2001 when he came down with emphysema on flight back from New York, an illness that he could never shake off. After five years of being almost permanently confined to a wheelchair, Freddie Garrity died in May 2006. He was sixty-nine and despite the pain he must have endured he was laughing and joking to the last. He may not have been the most gifted musician in the world, nor the greatest singer, but he achieved his dream of pop stardom. And thanks to his irrepressible personality and sense of fun he gave people the greatest gift of all: laughter. It is not a bad legacy.

*

If Freddie Garrity's looks were of no help in his rise to the top of the pop world, the same couldn't be said of Peter Noone. With his bee-stung lips, floppy hair and boyish charm he was the Justin Bieber of his day. Like Bieber he was irresistible to teenage girls, who turned out in their thousands for his concerts. With a genius for a record producer – the late, great Mickie Most – Noone and the band he led, Herman's Hermits, were almost certain to enjoy huge success. And huge it was: the Hermits had eighteen top-forty hits in the US and a similar number in the UK, including many that went to number one.

Although neither of his parents had any involvement in showbiz – they were both accountants – it seemed that Noone was destined for the life from an early age. Born in Davyhulme in 1947, he studied voice and drama at St Bede's College and then moved to the Manchester School of Music, where he was honoured by being named the outstanding young musician. But it was in the world of acting that he got his first break, as he explains.

> I was at Manchester School of Music trying to become a musician. One day someone came to the school looking for some kids to be on the telly in *Knight Errant*. I was chosen and then for another show . . . *Family Solicitor* I think. And so on and so on, and then *Coronation Street*. I played Stanley Fairclough and remember little other than the incredible professionalism of the assembled cast. When I forgot my lines, which was often, one of the old crew would say them in their speech and off I would go looking like an actor. This has stood me in good stead.

Despite this flirtation with acting, music was his first love. He was in a band called the Cyclones before leaving them and joining another combo, the Heartbeats. It wasn't long before Herman's Hermits was formed and with Most in the driving seat the hits started to flow. Their breakthrough came in 1964 when 'I'm Into Something Good' went to number one in the British charts. The songs that followed can best be described as bubblegum pop, but it was bubblegum pop of the highest order: 'Silhouettes', 'No Milk Today', 'There's a Kind of Hush', 'Something's Happening', 'Sunshine Girl', 'My Sentimental Friend', were just some of the cuts that made the top ten.

It was the same story in America where, on occasion, records that did not appeal to British fans made it into the higher reaches of the charts. 'Can't You Hear My Heartbeat' and 'Mrs Brown You've Got a Lovely Daughter' are good examples of this: they did nothing on this side of the Atlantic, but stormed to number one in the States. The Hermits' impact across the pond seemed to eclipse even their huge success in Britain. In fact in April 1965 the band had no less than three records in the American top twenty. Given this catalogue of hits, *Melody Maker* can hardly be accused of hyperbole for describing Herman's Hermits as 'the biggest British thing in America since the Beatles'. We should also not forget the extreme youth of the man fronting the Hermits: in 1965, Peter Noone was just eighteen years old.

The reaction to their live performances was even more enthusiastic. Their tour of the States in 1965 was on a par with Beatlemania at its peak, as Noone told *Melody Maker* after a gig in the Philadelphia convention centre.

> None of us can believe what happened here. There were 15,000 people there in that huge place. Actually, every night has been bigger than the last . . . We're not as famous in England, although we have had hit records there.
>
> They like us at home I guess but we don't get screamed at with thousands of kids pulling at our hair. And every night we get hundreds of cakes and presents brought to us backstage. It's fabulous.

The unstoppable rise of Herman's Hermits was not to everyone's taste. An ongoing rivalry developed with another British group: none other than the Rolling Stones. The Stones were also on the bill at the Philly convention centre and a dispute about who should go on stage last (the spot reserved for headliners) broke out between the two management teams. After tense negotiations it was agreed that the Hermits would go on first, but only after a forty-five minute break, which made it seem like two different shows.

Although the problem between the two acts appeared to have been resolved, it left a bitter aftertaste. According to Peter Noone, the Stones snubbed him and his band-mates. Then when a clearly irked Mick Jagger was asked for his views on his fellow Brits, he wasted no time in putting the boot in. 'I wish people would stop asking us what we think of them. We don't think of them at all. We think their music is weak and watery and not very significant.'

We can be sure the attitude of rival bands did not bother Peter Noone and his Hermits. They were too busy making monster hits, appearing on the leading television shows and performing live to hordes of screaming fans. Such was their status that on one tour of America they were backed by The Who, then an up-and-coming outfit but virtually unknown outside the London club scene. Along the way they met Elvis Presley, who surprised them by putting on an impromptu performance of one of their biggest hits 'I'm Henry the Eighth, I Am'. Presley may have been taking the proverbial, but Noone saw it as a compliment. 'He was making fun of me, but who cares. It was Elvis,' he said.

Away from the recording studio and the concert hall, Peter Noone lapped up the rock-and-roll lifestyle. He went drinking with The Beatles, to the Ad Lib club in London, where 'John Lennon would buy my drinks because he knew I was only sixteen and I wouldn't get drunk and try to beat somebody up'. Drinking was something he did, he says, to 'fit in. I wanted to be liked and didn't feel that interesting.' But what was originally designed to lubricate awkward social situations became a problem; in fact, an addiction. At the tender age of nineteen he attended a meeting of Alcoholics Anonymous, accompanied by his dad, who was also a heavy drinker. He decided to cut down and later gave up alcohol for good.

Lucky for him there was a stabilising influence in his life: Mireille, whom he married in 1968. The couple met in Ibiza.

> I think it was probably love at first lust with Mireille. Then I found out how nice she was and it turned to love. She kept turning me down,

but she was holidaying on Ibiza with her mum, so I rented the apartment next to them. Her mother liked me because I was respectful. I wore Mireille down.

They have been married for forty-five years – remarkable in the music business – and have a daughter. Thanks to his charm and youthful good looks, Noone has enjoyed a steady career in various branches of entertainment since Herman's Hermits split up in 1971. He has not only made many appearances on Broadway but has also guest-starred in several popular television shows in the United States, where he lives. For four years he hosted the highly rated *My Generation* on music station VHS, which was devoted to acts from the Sixties and Seventies, and later was a mentor on talent show *American Idol*. He also tours extensively with the Hermits and in 2011 went solo for a raft of British dates with the popular *Solid Silver 60s Show*.

It has been quite a career, made even more impressive by his early rise to stardom. Because of his age many wrote him off – 'Being 15, everyone thought I was just a schoolboy hottie and that I would have two hits and then go away' – but his staying power has proved to be remarkable.

8

DEATH ON THE RUNWAY

At 6.12 a.m. on 22 August 1985, British Airtours flight 28M began its takeoff at Manchester Airport. Thanks to a deadly chain of events about to unfold it was just thirty-six seconds from disaster. For those on board, it was the beginning of a nightmare many would never escape from as fate conspired against them.

As the Boeing 737 left the departure gate, the 130 or so passengers settled in their seats for the four-hour flight to the Greek island of Corfu. The prospect of hot summer sunshine at the end of the journey meant the atmosphere in the cabin was jovial and relaxed. Families and young couples made up the majority of the passenger list, and, having already been up since the early hours of the morning in preparation for the flight, some were already getting ready to grab a few hours' sleep.

British Airtours was a subsidiary of British Airways and offered cheap flights and package holidays in a bid to compete in the no-frills end of the market. The passengers were mostly from Manchester, but there was also a smattering of travellers from across the north-west. With the end of the school holidays still a fortnight away, it was peak season at Ringway – as the airport was then called – and the terminal building was packed with people preparing to fly around the globe. Just a normal morning at a busy provincial airport, but for those watching from the departure lounge their worst fears were about to unfold. As the 737 gathered speed, it suddenly billowed out thick black smoke and flames from the left-hand engine.

Inside the aircraft, as a speed of 140 miles per hour was reached, a loud thud was heard by everyone on board. Critically, Captain Peter

Terrington, 39, and senior first officer Brian Love, 51, with more than twenty thousand hours of flying time between them, heard it too. Believing there had been a tyre blow-out, or perhaps a bird strike, they decided to abort takeoff, gradually slowing the plane down while reporting their actions to the tower.

'Affirmative, there's fire, too. Lots of it. They're on their way,' was the terse response from air-traffic control.

The terrified passengers knew something very serious had happened. To those in the rear and on the left of the aircraft, it quickly became apparent it wasn't a tyre bursting or a bird strike because the flames spewing from the engine were now clearly visible. Air-traffic control advised exiting from the right-hand side and Captain Terrington informed the cabin crew to prepare for evacuation.

What had been initially thought of a rare problem, but one that was relatively easy-to-deal with, had now taken a sinister turn. Terrington knew every second would be crucial and he talked his number two through a gradual, though not instantaneous, halt. Stopping a fully loaded plane at high speed could have grave implications for the undercarriage so the aborted takeoff had to be carefully managed. The captain also knew that an engine fire on an aircraft with fully laden fuel tanks was perilous, but completely survivable. If the evacuation went to plan, there was no reason why everyone on board should not successfully escape. A member of the cabin crew went into the cabin to advise passengers about the evacuation, asking everyone to stay calm.

As the plane came to a standstill, fate played its hand. Terrington decided to pull off the runway at an exit on the right, close to the fire station. In many ways, it was a brilliant, split-second decision in a critical situation, but by stopping the plane where he did, the burning engine was now in the path of a gentle breeze. Although the wind speed was no more than two or three knots it still had a devastating effect. The flames were now being fanned across and below the rear cabin, rendering the rear doors on either side unusable while having the effect of a huge blow torch pointed at the back of the aircraft.

At first none of the passengers moved, partly because they were not sure what to do and partly because someone had shouted 'Calm down, sit down, everything will be okay.' To this day the person barking out these instructions has never been identified but one thing is certain: the instructions to stay put were the opposite of what should have happened; the evacuation had to begin as quickly as possible if the maximum number of lives were to be saved.

Within a very short space of time the passengers had no choice: the combination of heat and thick, black smoke quickly became unbearable and they took matters into their own hands. People stood up and moved up the aisle. At the front, purser Arthur Bradbury wrestled with the front right-hand door, which was jammed. He gave up on it and instead tried the left-hand door, which, to his relief, opened first time. After judging the fire was at a reasonable distance, the forward stewardess, Joanna Toff, began the evacuation procedure. First, she had to free a human jam in the twenty-two-inch aperture between the forward bulkheads and the door, grabbing a young boy in a yellow T-shirt and pulling him forward with force. This enabled those trapped there and behind to move freely again and people began to escape down the evacuation slide.

The airport fire service had taken just twenty-five seconds to reach the plane and sprayed thick foam as the terrified passengers slid down the chute. Bradbury, refusing to give up on the right-hand door, returned to his task and this time successfully opened it. After judging it was safe to do so, he successfully deployed the slide and began ushering passengers out. Another stewardess managed to open the right-hand aft door, but the inferno of fire and smoke made it impossible to use. On the other side, two young girls sitting next to the left-hand aft exit in row ten, attempted to open the forty-eight-pound door. It eventually pivoted on its lower edge and fell in, pinning one of the girls in her seat as the toxic black smoke billowed forward. A man behind freed her and removed the door to a spare seat, thus allowing more people to escape.

The thick smoke now engulfing the aircraft was deadly. With a consistency similar to an OXO cube it cut off the oxygen supply to the lungs with the result that one mouthful could be fatal. It meant the fate of those who had been sitting at the rear, and had not made it at least halfway along the aisle, was sealed. People couldn't stir themselves once they had taken a breath and although a few escaped from the left-hand aft exit, there were dozens who couldn't move. Although fresh air and safety were no more than a few feet away, they collapsed and, in turn, blocked the path of those behind. The rear of the fuselage was by now a raging inferno and the windows began to melt as flames licked through the air-conditioning grilles.

One passenger – Keith Middleton, 21, from Walton in Liverpool – was at the front of the plane and was later able to give an account of the nightmarish scene inside the stricken aircraft.

> Flames were billowing into the plane and I could not breathe. It was just a thick-black-smoke-filled aeroplane. Everyone was screaming and shouting and running here, there and everywhere. They were diving out of their seats and everyone was pushing.
>
> People were falling on the floor and getting trampled on. One of the stewards grabbed me and threw me down one of the chutes. It was like a scene from hell. People were trying to get out of the windows and running down the plane as fast as they could.

Anna Findlay of Bingley, West Yorkshire confirmed the initial indecision and also the subsequent mood of panic but thanks to a strong survival instinct she also made it to safety.

> Time just stood still and we watched the fire and didn't know what to do. No one moved initially. When they moved most of the people got trampled on. If we hadn't panicked more people would have got out . . . I went over the seats and just fought my way out.

John Beardmore, who miraculously got out with his wife and two children, survived after crawling towards the exit.

> I was just engulfed in this black smoke, toxic smoke that rolled down the cabin and with just one intake of it, my knees just buckled. It was so thick; it tasted of kerosene and plastic. You knew that if you got to inhale it a second time you would collapse.

Another survivor, Mike Mather, who was twenty-one at the time, said: 'Many did not stand a chance. The aisles of those planes are so small. People were just on top of each other trying to get out.' His words paint a ghastly picture of the final moments inside the aircraft.

As with all tales of disaster, accounts of twists of fate and heroism emerged in the days that followed the tragedy. William Beckett's daughter, Sarah, 18, was flying on her own for the first time and was due to take a job as a nanny on Corfu when she died in the tragedy. Incredibly, she had already had a brush with death earlier in the day. 'When you take one person away from the family it leaves a huge void and the whole chemistry of the family changes,' recalled her devastated father. 'It is desperately difficult to adjust and to come to terms with. You manage, but it's always there.' It seems Sarah's fate was sealed from the moment she awoke on that dreadful day, with her father revealing he was nearly involved in a head-on crash as he drove his daughter to the airport. 'I sometimes think what might have happened if we had crashed and been unable to get to the airport,' he said, solemnly. The family trauma was made worse in the aftermath with Sarah's death not officially confirmed for five long and painful days.

Survivor Lindsay Davies, of Sale, Manchester found a renewed zest for life in the wake of the disaster. Refusing to dwell on what might have been she instead adopted an attitude of hope and now makes the most of each day: 'It has changed my life but very positively,' she said. 'I am the most outgoing, optimistic, laid back and happy person. I realise you could be there one minute and gone the next.'

No matter how they managed to get out, the survivors all agreed on one point: the bravery and devotion to duty of the aircrew. Stewardess Joanna Toff continued to drag passengers to the escape slide as the inferno raged outside, including a young girl who had been trampled underfoot in the stampede. Several times Toff crawled back into the smoke-filled cabin in search of people trapped or injured, at considerable risk to her own life. Eventually, the heat and smoke became unbearable, and, barely able to breathe, she reluctantly left the aircraft. She was later awarded the Queen's Gallantry Medal for bravery (as was Arthur Bradbury, who also saved many lives). The plucky hostess is no longer working in the industry and has since married; now Joanna Caston, she lives in France with her family. The pilots also made it: first officer Love and then Captain Terrington exited through the sliding windows in the flight deck via a fabric escape strap.

Two of their colleagues were not so lucky. Jacqueline Urbanski, aged twenty-three and from Wardle, perished in the inferno. She had longed for a career in the skies, working for years as a clerk in the Rochdale tax office before realising her dream. Fellow stewardess Sharon Ford, a 22-year-old from Chesterfield, had a similar desire to work in the industry. She had returned to work just two days before the fatal flight, after a holiday in San Francisco. Her parents' heartbreak must have been made even worse when her 'postcard from beyond the grave' arrived from America shortly after she succumbed to the flames.

As the fire appliances on the outside gradually quelled the inferno, fire-fighters were able to go on board and carry out a search. When they saw bodies piled up in the aisles they immediately realised that survivors would be few and far between. However, one 14-year-old boy had a miraculous escape when the driver of a fire engine spotted his hand moving above a body in one of the over-wing exits and jumped onto the wing and dragged him to safety some five minutes and thirty seconds after the flames had taken hold. Twenty-five minutes later another man was discovered alive, but in a critical condition. He would die six days later in hospital as a result of his injuries.

Eddie Trimble, the engineering, evacuation and survival expert for the Air Accident Investigation Branch (AAIB) explained why so many had succumbed in the conflagration.

> Manchester is typical of what happens when an aircraft cabin is seriously affected by combustion products from cabin interior materials. The main problem is one of debilitation, a rapid reduction in your mobility which increases your time of exposure. The toxic gasses – carbon monoxide, hydrogen cyanide, acidic gasses, hydrogen chloride and hydrogen fluoride – affect your ability to use oxygen. Carbon monoxide combines with the haemoglobin and reduces the capability of the blood to transport oxygen to the tissues. Cyanide affects the tissues themselves and the more you breathe in, the more debilitated you become. It's a rapid process. This is why we found large groups of people who just hadn't the energy to make it.

The majority of aviation accidents take an age to investigate because, of course, most involve crashes that render debris into minute pieces, spread over a wide area. Manchester was much more straightforward and perhaps one of the simplest investigations in that the evidence was still largely intact and the vital pieces of the jigsaw were easily discovered.

The findings, however, were no less disturbing and the accident became the most influential event in the story of air safety, resulting in numerous recommendations that improved procedures for millions of air travellers.

Though much of the rear fuselage (which collapsed) was destroyed in the inferno, investigators quickly identified a tear in the access panel on the underside wing and a gaping hole in the combustion section of the left-hand engine. It begged the question: had the engine ruptured and blown a hole in the wing? There seemed no other explanation and AAIB engineering and power-plant expert, Steve Moss, who initially suspected that was the cause, had his hunch confirmed.

> We found that the combustion chamber outer case had actually split open. There are nine combustion cans in the combustion chamber outer case, arranged in a ring around the centre of the engine and fuel is injected in at high pressure. It then ignites and comes out the back of the can. Normally, you wouldn't be able to see any of them – they would be buried inside the combustion chamber outer case – but we could see virtually all the cans. The significant part of the can – and quite a heavy part, a cast piece known as the dome – was missing.

The part in question was discovered lying on the runway. It had struck the underside of the fuel-tank access panel after being spat out of the engine under tremendous force when the combustion chamber ruptured. The fracture it caused in the panel caused hundreds of gallons of fuel to spew out in the plane's wake with the heat from the engine blast igniting the fuel as it poured out.

Moss continued.

> Had it struck the wing, it probably wouldn't have penetrated the structure because it's quite strong, but the access panel is made of fairly brittle material and is really only there to keep the fuel in and therefore prone to impact damage of the type it sustained on takeoff. It had not really been foreseen that a part could actually come out of the combustion chamber and rupture one of those panels. Historically, there had been three occasions when parts, including the dome, had been ejected from JT8 engines and in those cases, take-off had been abandoned, fortunately without damage or loss of life. It was just very bad luck that it struck the under-wing access panel.

Answers were demanded on behalf of the families of the dead. There should have been enough time for everyone to escape, even if the fire and smoke had quickly spread. The AAIB identified a number of concerns in the official report, number 8/1988. It revealed that the engine that had caused the disaster, a Pratt & Whitney JT8D-15, had experienced previous cracks to the no. 9 combustor can, but it had been repaired. Critically, the repairs by welding were unsatisfactory in ensuring safe operation, contributing to the final severe cracking that led to the accident. The report also concluded that the positioning of the plane when it came to a halt contributed to the intensity of the fire, with even the gentlest of breezes having a devastating effect.

So why did fifty-five people die in what was, by all accounts and historically, a survivable accident, even if the fire had been ferocious? It should be noted that British Airtours, a subsidiary of British Airways, had an excellent safety record, and had not lost a single passenger since its formation fifteen years earlier. AAIB investigator-in-charge Dave King argued that a certain fatalistic attitude did not help.

> What shocked everyone about Manchester is that this aircraft didn't actually crash. It just decelerated under control on a very well-equipped airport, and came to a halt. Yet the fire managed to gain a hold so quickly that fifty-five people lost their lives.
>
> That placed a focus on survivability, something that, prior to 1985, if one looks at accident reports, was not a big issue. I don't know whether it was that perhaps we did accept that if you crashed aeroplanes it would inevitably have fatal consequences. I think now we are a little more enlightened.

There was also an issue about the number of passengers on board. Many experts felt that the number, which exceeded 130, was too high. The logjam of passengers in the middle of the plane was due to the fact the doors at the back of the plane were engulfed in flames and therefore unusable, but the over-wing exits were difficult to escape from and the reason may have been overcrowding. The standard model of the 737 used for scheduled flights seated 115 people but the package-holiday version, operating on tighter profit margins, had seats placed closer together to accommodate another fifteen people. Row ten in particular was deemed a contributory factor in delaying the evacuation. There simply wasn't

Robert Donat (*right*) as Mr Chipping, 'Chips', in the film *Goodbye Mr Chips*. Donat won the 1939 Academy Award for best actor thanks to his brilliant portrayal of the schoolmaster. The Manchester-born actor beat such luminaries as Clark Gable, James Stewart and Laurence Olivier to the Oscar.

(© Getty Images)

SOCCER AIR TRAGEDY

Manchester United plane crashes

22 dead

AN Elizabethan airliner, on charter to the fabulous Manchester United football team, crashed in flames at Munich Airport, Germany, yesterday, and plunged the world of Soccer into mourning.

Last night twenty-two men—among them some of the brightest stars in British football—were feared to have died in the crash.

Seven of them were members of the champion Manchester United football team—such international stars as Roger Byrne, the team captain, and centre forward Tommy Taylor.

Twenty-two of the forty-four people aboard the plane survived, including Matt Busby, the team's famous manager, two air hostesses and a baby.

Among those who died was Archie Ledbrooke, the Mirror's famous Northern sports writer.

● THE CRASH—Story and pictures: Back Page.
● THE TEAM in the Tragedy—See Centre Pages.

THE END The chartered Elizabethan airliner in which the Manchester United team was travelling home lies shattered in a snowfield near Munich. The pilot, Captain James Thain, escaped alive from the smashed nose (on the left of the picture).

THE BEGINNING This picture was taken when the team, accompanied by sports writers, boarded the plane at Manchester on Monday. Left to right, with known survivors marked with asterisk: Jackie Blanchflower*; Billy Foulkes*; Walter Crickmer, secretary; Don Davies, Manchester Guardian; Roger Byrne, captain; Duncan Edwards*; Albert Scanlon*—just visible behind Scanlon is Frank Swift, News of the World; Ray Wood*; Denis Viollet*; Archie Ledbrooke, Daily Mirror; Geoff Bent; Mark Jones and Alf Clarke, Kemsley Newspapers.

—Blackest Day of—
All—By Peter Wilson
—See Page 23—

The *Daily Mirror* front page of 7 February 1958, reporting that the plane carrying the legendary Busby Babes had crashed. The Munich Disaster, as it became known, made headlines around the world.

(© Mirrorpix)

Peter Noone, aka Herman, lead singer of Herman's Hermits. Thanks to a string of catchy songs and his boyish good looks, Noone and his band enjoyed incredible success both in Britain and America, and for a time even outsold The Beatles.

(© Mirrorpix)

Neville Cardus: the greatest cricket writer of them all

Clockwise from top left: Neville aged four; his mother Ada; the *Manchester Guardian* cricket correspondent; his editor on the *Guardian*, the great C. P. Scott; Neville Cardus towards the end of his life; his wife, Edith Cardus.

L. S. Lowry, the 'People's Painter', at an exhibition devoted
to his work in Salford in 1961. He is sitting in front of his
painting of Piccadilly Circus, London. Lowry is now accepted
by most good judges an artistic genius.

(© Mirrorpix)

above: Ten people lost their lives in the Irk Valley rail disaster of 1953. A catalogue of human errors led to tragedy.

below: The last major accident at Manchester Airport, in August 1985, on a flight to the holiday paradise of Corfu, caused the deaths of fifty-five holidaymakers and crew. The accident led to a root-and-branch review of aircraft safety procedures.

(© Mirrorpix)

Manchester's most eccentric pub: Tommy Ducks, demolished in 1993 after more than a century of insanity.

Elephant ride at Belle Vue, the 'Showground of the World'. Belle Vue, a Manchester institution, is much missed.

left: The great George Formby, star of several movies for Mancunian Films, with 'his little ukulele in his hand'.
(© Getty Images)

below: John E. Blakeley, movie-maker extraordinaire and the man behind Mancunian Films.

Trevor Hardy, the 'Beast of Manchester'. In a fifteen-month period during the mid-1970s, Hardy murdered three teenage girls before he was caught, prosecuted and given a life sentence.

(© Mirrorpix)

enough room for people to squeeze through quickly and it also meant there were initial problems in removing the door. As a result, the AAIB recommended that all row-ten seats be removed from 737s.

The AAIB also recommended the introduction of smoke hoods, which, on flight 28M, would have enabled many passengers to breathe and see more clearly, saving many lives as a result. Another recommendation was to widen the opening to the bulkhead galley, where several people had become locked together and unable to move in the stampede to escape. Procedures were also put in place to ensure that flight crew were aware that the positioning of the aircraft should be downwind of the fuselage when involved in a fire. To assist pilots, external indicators that would show the local wind direction were suggested. Water-mist sprays, fire extinguishers to be stored at cabin-crew stations and a host of other amendments that could save lives were all put forward and introduced, though it took years to implement them.

There were other factors on the awful day in question that may have cost lives. Seemingly random, isolated events that, when strung together, formed a lengthy list: faulty water hydrants; the repainting and initial unavailability of the major airport foam tender; failure of the relevant authorities to notify the airport police of a change in procedure regarding external emergency vehicles. There was also a delay in the external fire chief locating the airport fire chief to hand over control. In addition, Monnex – a powder that could have stopped the burning fuel streaming out onto the concrete and creating a flaming pool under the plane – was available on the airport fire engines, but not used because of lack of recent training. The list seemed endless.

Though the airport fire crew and external fire crew undoubtedly saved lives, the AAIB report could not rule out the possibility that, had everything been working perfectly and been available to the crews when it was needed, more lives could have been saved. It was time for a root-and-branch review, as Dave King acknowledged.

> We didn't manage to evacuate the people quickly enough. So we felt it was our challenge to examine the evacuation criteria, look at all of the protection to stop fire rapidly penetrating such a fuselage and look at the research that had predicted that the fuselage would be better at penetrating such fire penetration.

The people who perished did not die in vain. Today, air travel is much safer thanks to the lessons learnt on that fateful day in August 1985 and fires similar to the one that devastated flight 28M would likely have a much higher survival rate. Yet one recommendation that AAIB investigator Eddie Trimble suggested – smoke hoods – still hasn't been adopted. The reason? Almost certainly cost. Today, Trimble carries his own smoke hood in his hand luggage on every flight he takes.

The flight 28M disaster remains Manchester Airport's worst aviation accident and in August 2010 a memorial service was organised to mark the twenty-fifth anniversary of the disaster. Since the fateful day, there have been no more fatalities. Let us pray it stays that way.

9

THE MANCHESTER EXPRESS

Shortly before the death of a patient, the doctor treating him at Crumpsall Hospital said to a nurse: 'See that fellow over there? He thinks he was a world champion. Don't they come up with some fantastic stories?'

The nurse replied, 'Actually, he was. And from what I'm told, he was one of the greatest.'

They were talking about Jackie Brown, the Manchester Express; the city's first world champion. Brown was idolised during the 1930s, a time when he had the boxing world at his feet. However, even during his glory days his life was touched by tragedy and controversy. It is a compelling story of rags to riches and riches to rags, peppered by moments of great triumph and deep despair. Many people have observed that it would make a great film and they are right because the Jackie Brown story has everything.

He came into the world on 29 November 1909 at 18 Armour Street in Collyhurst, an area known as Little Ireland because of the number of people who could trace their heritage to the Emerald Isle. He was the youngest of five children and although it was a happy upbringing, life was far from easy for the Browns. Like most of their neighbours their house had no electricity and they relied on a coal fire for heat and gas mantles for light. They were overcrowded and the only toilet facilities were outside in the back yard, a grim prospect in the depths of winter. Collyhurst was one of the poorest neighbourhoods in the country and the streetscapes reflected that fact: all around there were cotton mills, factories and warehouses and there was always the looming presence of Strangeways prison in the distance. During the colder months, the endless smoking chimneys gave the damp air a pungent, charred aroma that frequently turned to thick 'pea-souper' fogs.

There was something about the lightly built Brown during his days at St Patrick's – a Roman Catholic school on Livesey Street – that set him apart. Small in stature, he was often the target of older boys who preyed on anyone perceived to be weak. They thought he could be pushed around, and, although his gift of the gab helped to extricate him from a few tight spots, Jackie realised that he needed more than a silver tongue. So he learned how to box, shrewdly utilising his physical attributes: he was nimble, quick-footed and he discovered that despite his light frame he could pack a punch if he focused his energy into his fists. Before long, the bullies gave him a wide berth and those who didn't invariably ended up with a bloody nose.

In his early teens, he joined the Collyhurst & Moston Lads' Boxing Club where his rougher edges were honed. After earning the princely sum of twelve shillings for beating Arthur Evitt in promoter Len Johnson's canvas-topped 'blood tub' a few miles from his home, the plucky 16-year-old decided this was no hobby. He wanted to make a career in the ring and while his first purse was a pittance, it promised an escape from an endless line of dead-end jobs. To begin with, boxing was a means to an end. It helped put food on the table and enabled him to have the independence he desired, but as he continued to get the better of his opponents and his winnings grew larger, he dreamt of fame and fortune and a life a million miles away from the one his parents had long since accepted as their lot.

Len Johnson had been a talented boxer and was himself a fascinating character. Born in Manchester in 1902, the son of William Johnson, an African merchant seaman and a Mancunian girl, Margaret Maher, he followed his father into amateur boxing. After turning professional in 1922, he beat some of the best British and foreign fighters of the day as a middleweight. However, his black skin had cruelly denied him the opportunity of fighting for a Lonsdale belt with the boxing authorities ruling that only whites could contest official title fights.

Instead, Johnson was left to earn a meagre living from the talent of others. He saw a bright future for Jackie but racial prejudice meant he could only take his protégé so far. Nevertheless, he did all he could to further the young man's development and pointed him in the direction of 'Kid' Furness's boxing booth on Rochdale Road, just yards from Brown's home. Furness, also a former boxer, was the epitome of the street-smart promoter, putting on seven boxing shows a week all over Lancashire, Cheshire and Derbyshire. He was a hard taskmaster and he would often reduce the promised purse if a boxer failed to put on a good show. Jackie Brown would have many run-ins with Furness over money, noting ruefully that the promoter could 'peel an orange without taking his hands out of his pockets'.

At first he would have nothing to do with the scrawny teenager. Jackie would go along to Furness's promotions and cheekily challenge his fighters. The great boxing impresario was not amused, telling Brown, 'Go away. You're much too young, besides you're too little. You'll get yourself killed.' In the end Jackie wore Furness down and by the age of sixteen the young prospect from Collyhurst was taking on all-comers and beating them. Furness soon realised he was dealing with a fighter who 'was fantastically brilliant . . . a master craftsman and one of the best boxers ever'. He was less complimentary about Jackie Brown's character. 'As a person . . . no comment,' he would later tell an interviewer.

Word quickly spread about Jackie's prowess and before long he was packing them in on Rochdale Road. Collyhurst was a boxing hotbed, with around twenty gyms and Furness made good money from Brown. However, like Johnson, he realised he could only take the young man so far. So, when he lost him to the stable of Harry Fleming, a manager who was making a big name for himself, Furness was pragmatic and accepted the loss of his star fighter.

Brown's first professional fight took place on 18 May 1925 when, still aged sixteen, he beat Harry Gainey on points. The plucky youngster had passed his first serious test and was on his way. As more bouts followed it became clear this was a real talent. Although he did not have a big punch he had incredible speed, which made it very difficult for other boxers to lay a glove on him, and this was allied to perfect balance and a great boxing brain. The pugilistic ability was complemented by dark good looks, an abundance of charm and a desire to entertain the people who came to see him. It is little wonder that promoters were desperate to get the man dubbed the Manchester Express on their bills.

Before long a crack at the British flyweight title beckoned. He was scheduled to take on Bert Kirby, from Birmingham, in a final eliminator, with the winner qualifying to meet the stylish Scot, Johnny Hill, who was then British champion. In the interim, however, Hill died, which meant that the bout with Kirby would now be for the title. The Brummie boxer was a tough cookie and much more experienced than the 20-year-old Brown. He would also have the considerable advantage of fighting on home turf with promoter Ted Salmon organising the clash at a West Bromwich skating rink. The men who lay the odds – and bookies rarely get it wrong – made Kirby the red-hot favourite.

None of that fazed Jackie Brown. This was the opportunity he craved and in front of a packed house (and thousands more outside), he took the fight to Kirby, showing speed and agility. Both fighters went for broke in the first two rounds and there was little to separate them going into the third. Brown then upped the ante, sensing he might have the measure of his opponent. Kirby, however, inspired by his home crowd, battled back bravely but Brown saw an opening and landed a punch flush on Kirby's chin, laying him out flat. The fight was over and Jackie Brown was the flyweight champion of Britain, earning £95 in the process.

The effect on the cities of Birmingham and Manchester was incredible. It has to be remembered that the British title meant something really special in those days and the build-up to the fight had been avidly followed by everyone in the Midlands and the north-west. Such was the emotion generated by the bout that when it was over scuffles broke out all over the arena. The scenes outside, where an estimated ten thousand ticketless fans had gathered, were even worse, with some describing what happened as a riot. The violence may have been sparked by a clash of heads in that fateful third round, which left Kirby groggy, and led to claims from the home support that Brown had deliberately butted his opponent.

Despite the trouble after the fight, all that the people of Manchester cared about was that one of their own was the champion and when the news reached the city there were wild celebrations on the streets and in the pubs. Brown got home to Collyhurst later that night and found there were hundreds waiting to congratulate him. The clamour was such that he agreed to an exhibition match a couple of days after the title win just so the Manchester public could express their appreciation. Jackie also found time to visit his old school, St Patrick's, where the four thousand pupils and their teachers had thrown a party to mark the achievement of their alumnus. The world was truly his oyster.

Although Brown lost a rematch with Kirby five months later he had clearly been unwell with flu-like symptoms. That meant a decider was needed and so the third Brown–Kirby fight in less than sixteen months was held at the King's Hall. Brown went into the fight in good form having won four of his last five fights, and, spurred on by the home crowd, he won on points. More glory was to follow. He was at his sparkling best as he added the European Boxing Union title later in the year after edging past Romanian Lucian Popesco with a hard-fought points victory at an ecstatic Belle Vue. The little man from Collyhurst was now on course to fight for the world title.

Out of the ring Jackie had met his match. Her name was Mary Chapman, who, like her husband-to-be, was from Collyhurst and had also attended St Pat's. On 19 October 1931, they got married at St Patrick's church amid chaotic scenes. Thousands packed the roads, church-yard and surrounding buildings to capture a glimpse of Manchester's favourite son and wish him good luck. Eventually, the police had to clear the roadway to ensure the bride and bridegroom actually made it to their own wedding on time! Film stars, footballers from both City and United, and other boxers, among them fellow Collyhurst legend Johnny King, were in attendance. Manager Harry Fleming was not only best man but also gave away the bride, whose father was deceased.

The reception at the Piccadilly cafe in the city centre was a glamorous affair. Speeches were made praising Jackie to the hilt for his boxing triumphs and when he was asked to respond he decided that a few words would not be enough. Brown strode confidently to the stage, spoke to the band and then with considerable joie de vivre belted out two popular songs: 'McNamara's Band' and 'Myra My Girl'. He brought the house down, with many comparing the ecstatic reception from the hundreds of wedding guests as akin to the atmosphere at one of his title fights. That was Jackie Brown all over; he loved the limelight and he loved to please the crowds.

Now at the peak of his powers he won a string of fights, including a British title defence against Jim Maharg at Belle Vue. It set up a match with Tunisian-born Victor 'Young' Perez, now representing France. Jackie Brown would be fighting for the flyweight championship of the world. Perez was, in many ways, similar to his Mancunian opponent. Brave as a lion and from a modest background, his burning ambition to be the best on the planet had inspired a rise to the top. A flamboyant ladies man, he posed a serious threat to Brown, but the Manchester Express had one big advantage: his vociferous home fans. The fight, on 31 October 1932, would be at the King's Hall, Belle Vue.

What happened that night lived up to expectations as both men gave everything. As they tired, the will of the 7,800 sellout crowd carried Brown when he needed it most, and, in the thirteenth round, the local hero landed a killer blow. A stunned Perez staggered and after yet another volley of punches, his team threw in the towel. The contest was over and the scrawny five-foot-five lad from Collyhurst was crowned champion of the world.

How the city, and especially Collyhurst, celebrated, as Brown recalled.

> I had a worse do with the neighbours than I had with Perez. They welcomed me home magnificently and would not let me get to bed until the early hours of the morning. I went to my brother's house farther down the street and it was even worse there. They threw confetti at me!

The triumph was not only Jackie Brown's, but also Manchester's. Even the milkman left a note on his gold top the next morning. 'Well done Jackie,' it proclaimed.

*

Away from the ring, Brown was bigger than Hollywood superstar Rudolph Valentino to the people of Manchester, mobbed wherever he went. To please his fans he played up to his image during fights and his showmanship almost cost him dear on a number of occasions, but, for the entertainer supreme, it was worth the risk. Jackie danced around the ring, winking every now and then to assure his public everything was under control. Before he gloved up he would run a comb through his mop of thick, black hair and, of course, the crowd lapped it up.

Until David Beckham came along, there has probably never been a more sartorially elegant sportsman. Brown was always immaculately turned out in the finest suits, which were invariably topped off by a trilby hat and a luxurious fur coat, the latter becoming something of a trademark. The car he drove was predictably flashy, an American Studie-Baker, but what made it unusual was the fact that he would be driven around Manchester by a chauffeur. The lad from the back streets now had a limo and a chauffeur. No wonder he attracted so much attention.

While many top boxers, fearing a return to the poverty-stricken life most of them had endured, were careful with their earnings Jackie spent as if there were no tomorrow. A big house was acquired, in the affluent Cheshire suburb of Bramhall, showing how far he had come from the hard-knock streets of Collyhurst. Jackie Brown was generous to a fault, both with his time and his money. He would spend hours signing autographs and stayed much longer than expected on his many visits to schools and youth clubs. And when he went back to Collyhurst in his flash motor he would dole out money to the elderly and buy all the kids in the area an ice cream.

Life however was not all sweetness and light. He drank heavily, often ending up in unseemly brawls with people who were only too pleased to have a punch-up with a world champion. It is also clear that he was a compulsive womaniser, although to be fair to him women would just not leave him alone after he won his titles. It was this dangerous cocktail of money, alcohol, natural aggression and desire that led to him becoming embroiled in two very serious incidents, both of which had the potential to end his glorious career in the ring.

The first saw him kill a woman, while the second ended with him being detained for four months at His Majesty's pleasure in Strange-ways prison.

It was a dismal autumnal Sunday in October 1933. The rain had been teeming down all day and the dark clouds above Manchester had turned day into night. Despite the awful weather Jackie Brown's disposition was distinctly sunny. He had everything: he was world boxing champion; he had a lovely wife and a baby daughter; and they lived in a beautiful house in the affluent Cheshire suburbs. Driving home from a visit to friends in Collyhurst he had but one thought in his mind – the party to celebrate the christening of his daughter Mary Jacqueline, which had taken place that day at his home parish of St Patrick's.

Bowling along without a care in the world, Brown turned into Bramhall Lane in Stockport. It was pouring with rain and the road was in a dangerous condition with deep puddles and limited visibility making driving conditions near impossible. Perhaps that was why he did not see Mrs Margaret Thornley cross the road. There was a terrible collision, in which the unfortunate lady was killed instantly. To his credit, Brown, not realising that she was already dead, immediately jumped out of his car, picked her up and drove straight to Stockport Infirmary.

There was an inquest the next day, at which the coroner heard two versions of events. Guy Thornley, the dead woman's husband, testified that in normal circumstances his wife would have had plenty of time to cross the road. The problem, he said, was that Brown had been driving at 'terrific speed'. Other witnesses gave conflicting accounts; one stated that the car had been travelling at a 'very high speed' while another told the court that its speed was 'moderate'. Another factor may have contributed to Mrs Thornley's death: several witnesses noted she was holding an umbrella in front of her face and may not have had a clear view of oncoming traffic.

Having heard the evidence the jury took only ten minutes to return a verdict. It found that the cause of death was Brown's negligent driving but that the negligence did not constitute manslaughter. Jackie Brown was said to be devastated by the accident, although this did not lead him to withdraw from his next fight, which took place just fifteen days later.

Jackie Brown's culpability for what happened in Bramhall Lane is debatable. However, there is no doubt about where blame should be apportioned for what happened on a Manchester street ten months later. On Sunday, 1 July 1934 he had been on a trip to Blackpool, and was drinking alone in a hotel bar. He saw his friend's wife, Vera Sheldon, whose nickname was Blondie, with two men and another woman and went over to ask what she was doing there. Not satisfied with the answer, and knowing Vera's husband was away working in London, he asked her to return to Manchester with him because he didn't like the company she was keeping, particularly as she had a young baby at home.

An altercation ensued between Brown and one of the men in the group: Louis Tarchman, an amateur boxer who Brown knew vaguely from the blood-tub days. Brown followed the party to their car and then tracked them all the way from Blackpool to Manchester. After stopping a traffic light in the city, Tarchman jumped out to confront the champion, who also got out of his car. The pair exchanged words and then the fisticuffs started. In the ensuing tussle, Brown bit part of his opponent's ear off. He would later claim Tarchman's low blow caused him to clench his teeth and that he had no intention of biting his ear. Brown was later arrested and despite his celebrity the authorities decided the case could not be dropped. World champion boxer or not, the law had to be applied.

A clumsy attempt was made by Brown's associates to buy off Tarchman but the promised payment of £200 did not materialise and the fact that a bribe had been offered would go against Brown when the court proceedings got under way. Perhaps more in hope than expectation he entered a plea of not guilty, but the evidence against him was overwhelming. After the trial at Manchester city quarter sessions the jury brought in a guilty verdict and he was given four month's hard labour by the Recorder, Sir Walter Greaves Lord, KC. By the standards of the day it was a lenient sentence; lesser mortals convicted of a similar offence would have been facing four or five years inside.

Brown later commented that he hoped others would do the same if they saw his wife in a similar situation. It was bizarre to say the least that he would go to such lengths to defend the reputation of his friend's wife, though a feud with Tarchman had been simmering for several years, with fuel being thrown on the flames when the latter told Brown prior to the altercation, 'Don't be so cocky. It's only four years ago since you were holding a bucket for me.' While there was no suggestion of a relationship between Jackie and Blondie, the whole affair must have taken some explaining to Mrs Brown.

Though his legion of fans was dismayed at his internment, they never lost faith and the general opinion was that he had been provoked and should have been found not guilty. The press didn't condemn him, either, knowing a fair proportion of their readers wouldn't entertain any criticism of their hero.

*

In Strangeways, Jackie worried about the reaction of his fans. How would they take to their hero being sent to prison for assault? They didn't seem to mind; in fact they were more adoring than ever before. At his comeback fight against Orlando Magliozzi some ten months later, a sell-out crowd of more than seven thousand gave him a rapturous reception. Touched by the love he was being shown, Brown thanked the people of Manchester for believing in him and helping get his career back on track. He saw off his opponent with a fourth round knockout.

Brown fought on, hungry to make up for lost time, but it was clear he was not the same man. Strangeways had not helped and his fitness was being affected by hard-living and late nights. He had managed to defend his world title on three occasions: twice against Frenchman Valentin Angelmann in 1933 and once against Chris Foran of Liverpool in the same year. But in a third meeting against Angelmann, in 1934, he was unconvincing, just managing to scrape a draw. It meant that he retained the world title but his faithful fans wondered for how much longer.

The following year, in September 1935, Jackie Brown met his nemesis.

His next opponent for the world title was to be one Benny Lynch, from Glasgow. There were many similarities between the two men. Both came from Irish Catholic backgrounds and both came from the toughest part of their respective cities. Lynch in fact was brought up in the place that has become a byword for street fighting and gang violence: the Gorbals. In terms of innate boxing ability, Lynch, like Brown, was right out of the top drawer: the little Glaswegian had won his last twenty-eight fights in a row, many of them by knockout. One top referee described the man from the Gorbals as the 'perfect fighting machine' while another official thought his left hook was the hardest punch he had ever seen on a flyweight.

Both Manchester and Glasgow were, and are, boxing mad and the hype for this one surpassed any fight that had ever taken place in the United Kingdom. The *Manchester Evening Chronicle*, with some justification, called it the 'fight of the century' while auditoria north and south of the border were desperate to stage it. But it was the King's Hall at Belle Vue that won the right with a huge purse offer of £3,800. Seven thousand tickets were snapped up with the promoters reckoning they could have sold many thousands more if the King's Hall had the required capacity.

Brown had taken on Lynch a few months earlier in a non-title fight in Glasgow and come away with a draw. He was therefore optimistic about his chances, although some boxing historians have speculated, controversially, that Lynch pulled his punches to ensure he would get a crack at Brown's titles. Whatever happened in that first fight, at Belle Vue there was only one man in it: the little Glaswegian floored Brown three times in the first round and five times in the second. To the dismay of the partisan home crowd the fight was stopped, and Lynch headed back across the border as world champion and national hero.

After the Lynch fight, Brown realised that he could no longer get down to the flyweight limit of eight stone without sapping his strength and so he made the decision to move up to bantamweight. Thanks to his sheer doggedness he climbed the rankings in the new division until he was named number-one contender for the British title. The problem was that the crown was held by his Harry Fleming stable-mate, Johnny King, who was also from Collyhurst. Fleming had seen the pair fight before in a non-title bout (which King won easily) and didn't want them to do it all over again, even if it was for a national championship. He did all he could to derail the bout but eventually the pair climbed into the ring at Belle Vue's speedway stadium, where the Collyhurst titans contested one of the most compelling and brutal fights of all time.

Watched by a record crowd for Manchester boxing of around twenty thousand – most of whom were hoping to see Jackie Brown recapture his former glories – it was an emotional evening for all concerned. Harry Fleming couldn't bear to watch and went to Blackpool for the day. It was the right decision because this wasn't a boxing match. It was a massacre.

Despite doing well in the early stages, Brown soon ran out of stamina and then had to endure round after round of vicious punches to the head and body. He could hardly raise his arms, much less defend himself, and only raw courage was keeping him on his feet. Many in the crowd, sickened by the punishment he was taking, howled at the referee to stop the fight. In the thirteenth round, the inevitable came to pass when King landed a knockout blow. It was heartbreaking to see such a great boxer unceremoniously dumped to the canvass and as Jackie was carried away from the ring, unconscious, Johnny King wept.

He wasn't the only one.

The *Daily Express*, while praising Brown's fortitude, was worried about the injuries he had sustained, noting that he 'was suffering from concussion and a possible fracture at the base of the skull and being attended by three doctors who were making efforts to revive him'. Many people, including his family, believe that his later heath problems stemmed from the savage beating he sustained at King's hands.

Yet he continued to box, simply because he needed the money, although it was now at a lower level and much less lucrative. His last officially sanctioned fight was against Benny Jones, on 24 July 1939. Fittingly, it was at Belle Vue, his spiritual home, and how the Manchester fans roared when he was declared the winner on points. They did not realise they would never again see their hero in action. Within a couple of weeks the Second World War had started and people had more to concern them than boxing. Jackie did his bit for the war effort, being stationed in France until 1941 as a PT instructor before being discharged on medical grounds.

The years that followed were difficult ones. He needed constant medical treatment and suffered from depression, a sad state of affairs for such a great athlete. Predictably, the hangers-on who had been legion in his heyday were now conspicuous by their absence. Apart from his loyal wife Mary and three children, he was effectively alone in the world and the fortune he earned in the ring – estimated to be in the region of £100,000–£150,000 – was a distant memory. He was not totally forgotten. Irish tenor Josef Locke attempted to ease Brown's financial burden, waiving his £150 fee for a Belle Vue benefit concert in aid of the down-on-his-luck boxer. However, the high cost of staging the event meant that Brown would have received nothing if it hadn't been for a collection on the night, which raised just shy of £90.

As the years rolled by, Jackie would stroll through the picturesque Boggart Hole Clough, a 190-acre park near Blackley, reminiscing about the days he had used the route for road work. Alcohol continued to dominate his life and there were many run-ins with the police, most of them occurring after his regular drinking sessions. Unable to work and with the little benefit he received insufficient to look after his wife and children, the Brown family had to give up their privately rented Blackley home in January 1964 and move into a council flat.

Little is known about what happened next in Jackie's life, but seven years later, on 15 March 1971, he died in the Crumpsall hospital where he had been resident for almost four years. At time of his death, Natt Basso, chairman of the Central Area Board of British Boxing Control, said: 'It would have been a joke for him to go in against any of today's fighters. Jackie Brown came from a time when he had to be great or he did not eat.'

Great he most certainly was. He lost 24 of his 141 professional fights, though it is estimated he fought closer to three hundred times when his amateur career is taken into account. It is quite a record, but then, Jackie Brown was quite a boxer. For Mancunians, he was the greatest.

10

THE REAL SHERLOCK HOLMES

Sir Arthur Conan did not base the hero of *The Hound of the Baskervilles* and *A Study in Scarlet* on Manchester detective Jerome Caminada, but it would have not been a surprise if his exploits had provided the inspiration for Sherlock Holmes. Both Caminada and Holmes used ingenious methods, including a range of disguises, to capture their quarry, and, but for the worldwide popularity of Conan Doyle's creation, Manchester's greatest sleuth would undoubtedly be the better known of the crime-fighting duo today.

Caminada took as much satisfaction in seeing a crooked coal merchant who made short deliveries placed behind bars as he did a callous killer. In his book, once you had broken the law, you had stepped over the line and were treated accordingly. You were a criminal, no matter the offence.

Born to Francis and Mary Caminada on 30 March 1844, he was registered initially under the name Ambrose, but, by the time of the christening his parents had changed their son's name to Jerome. He came from good, honest stock: his father an Italian immigrant and his mother an Irish Catholic. They lived and worked off Deansgate, opposite the Free Trade Hall, in the very heart of Manchester city centre and a stone's throw from the infamous 1819 Peterloo Massacre, the scene of one of the city's greatest injustices.

In those days, Deansgate was far from the prosperous hub it is today. It was a den of iniquity, crime-ridden and filled with tough pubs and brothels. It was the embodiment of Manchester's sinister underworld. Living there would have presented the sternest of tests for any young man trying to stay on the straight and narrow, but, fortunately for Jerome, he was raised in a God-fearing family with parents who wanted only the very best for their son. They sent him to St Mary's school on Mulberry Street, adjacent to the town hall, and the family worshipped at nearby St Mary's church, also known as 'The Hidden Gem'; it was, ironically, a place that criminals would come to worship Jerome, in a manner of speaking.

The young Caminada was a determined and conscientious lad and he was one of the few at school who could read and write, giving him a head start on his peers. After leaving school, he found gainful employment at Mather and Platts, an engineering firm in Salford. However, it wasn't long before he found his true calling when he became a member of the police reserve, a special constabulary of the day. Then, in February 1868, disillusioned with life as an engineer, Caminada began his love affair with law and order in earnest, when he joined Manchester constabulary at the age of twenty-four.

His first night on duty was to be something of a rude awakening: he was punched in the face by a hoodlum, who accused him of being 'a lazy copper,' not worth the taxes he paid. Constable Caminada arrested his attacker after a scuffle in which he sustained some minor, though painful, injuries.

Caminada was unperturbed by his baptism of fire. He had found his niche and he excelled in his new career, becoming a sergeant within three years and being transferred to the newly formed detectives division, based at the town hall. He was destined to become the scourge of Manchester's criminal fraternity and his distinct advantage was that he had been brought up in the toughest part of town. He knew where lawlessness flourished. Hadn't he been a witness to it every day of his young life? Where Jerome Caminada was concerned there were no boltholes or dark alleys in which crooks could escape the increasingly long arm of the law, because he knew every nook, cranny, back street and ginnel in central Manchester.

Policing was more than a job; more even than a vocation. It was to him nothing short of a moral crusade and he set about ridding the city of thieves, hustlers and murderers with a zeal that few could match. And he didn't just concentrate on the parasitical street criminals, such as muggers and pickpockets. He actively sought to uncover the more sophisticated fraudsters and conmen with his own self-styled under-cover operations, which were years ahead of their time. Caminada would do whatever it took to prove the guilt of those suspected of skulduggery, as several 'quacks' of the time quickly discovered.

Fuelled by reports of questionable medical practitioners in the Plymouth Grove area of Manchester, Caminada posed as a warehouse-man seeking help for his sweating palms. He made several appoint-ments with the fake practitioners, who were fleecing the local populace of hundreds of pounds. The results were comical as the detective quickly brought several 'experts' to task after uncovering them as no more than callous fraudsters. There was money to be made from medicine with people desperate to cure their ills by seeking the advice of these so-called private practitioners. The quacks' diagnosis would almost always lead to severe weight loss – of the patient's wallet – as they recommended that the only known cure was a concoction they just happened to have available, for a hefty price, of course.

Caminada, relatively unknown to the public, decided to put the conmen behind bars as a warning to others. He attended 'clinics' in Nelson Street, looking to cure his chest pain and sweaty palms.

'Are you guilty of self-pollution?' asked one, sternly.

'No, never,' replied Caminada.

'Urinate into this tumbler,' ordered the quack. 'I can tell if anything is the matter with you from that.'

Caminada refused.

'Have you £3 and I will give you a case of medicine which will put you right in five or six weeks?'

The charade became even more ridiculous. Eventually, Caminada left with a bottle of medicine and was advised to drink a wineglass of the stuff every day and to come back when he had finished the course. Tests proved the medicine to be nothing more than sarsaparilla, effectively a placebo. An arrest was made and the quack was fined £5. Others quickly followed. Here is a selection of remedies for the same ailment offered by the charlatans on Nelson Street. To cure his sweating palms, Caminada was advised to: take four steps; turn on the water-tap every morning; go to theatres; ride outside of omnibuses; not drink green tea; soak his head and shoulders and rub vigorously with a towel!

Caminada's reputation grew, to the extent that he became a target for Manchester's top criminals. Threats were made on his life and he carried a pistol in case of an assassination attempt. He wasn't over-reacting because from time to time he had cause to use the weapon.

His face became too well known to continue effective undercover work, so he began to use a variety of disguises to trap his prey, one of the many similarities to Sherlock Holmes and a very effective one. His cases became the stuff of legend and courthouses would be packed out to hear how he had ingeniously brought another crook to justice. Gasps could be heard as his methods were relayed to juries; for example, the time he hid inside a piano at the Free Trade Hall in order to capture a thief in the act.

Another favourite saw him stake out a hall on York Street after a tip-off about the bizarre activities of a group of men who occasionally met there. Caminada could overcome most obstacles and despite the hall having all but two of its windows screened from the outside world, he found a good vantage point from a rooftop opposite. Taking up a precarious viewing position from behind a chimney stack, Caminada witnessed enough criminal activity to warrant a raid. He witnessed the gathered men, many clad in female attire and several clearly involved in homosexual activity. They were dancing and cavorting, safe, or so they believed, in the knowledge that they were among their own and could break the law, as it then was, without fear of capture.

A dozen constables were summoned and when the signal was given Caminada knocked gently on the front door several times before a voice asked who was there. In a female tone, Caminada responded, 'Sister', the password for the evening, and as the door opened the police rushed in. They were soon under attack from men desperate, for obvious reasons, to avoid arrest but eventually officers overpowered them and wholesale arrests were made.

The prisoners, many still dressed in the gaudy attire they had been arrested in, were remanded in custody and appeared several days later in front of a packed courthouse. The public was eager to discover the identities of the defendants who were by now the talk of the town.

Caminada had noted that among those charged with 'gathering with the purpose to commit abominable offences,' were several male prostitutes. Fearing the accused would be attacked in jail, the judge acted leniently and fined the men heavily.

Perhaps the case that gave him most satisfaction involved the capture and conviction of a notorious criminal he had been after for more than twenty years. It was the early 1880s and every officer in Manchester was looking for the city's public-enemy-number-one: Bob Horridge. The incorrigible Horridge had robbed a shop in Rochdale Road, shooting two police officers in the process. Caminada knew that Horridge was an intelligent and resourceful career criminal who would not be easily apprehended. He would have to go above and beyond the call of duty to bring him to justice.

So Caminada, utilising his talent for disguise, dressed up as a labourer and began to tail 'Little Ada', as Horridge's wife was known. Sure enough she led him straight to Liverpool docks and her husband. It was at this point that the dedicated detective showed once again why he was so feared in the underworld. Caminada made a habit of studying not only the appearance of criminals but also their gait, often touring local prisons to observe them in the exercise yard. At the docks he saw Horridge from behind, striding away from him, and recognised the way he walked.

'Hello Bob. How are you?' Caminada asked, pressing his revolver against the villain's mouth. 'If there's any nonsense with you, you'll get the contents of this,' he cautioned, in his sternest tone.

Horridge wasn't about to come easily and after he reached for his own gun a violent struggle ensued. By this time, however, other police officers had come onto the scene and an arrest was made. After his trial Horridge got a life sentence and Caminada felt, with some justification, that it was a great day for law and order. 'When Horridge was sent to penal servitude for life, the public had the pleasure of knowing that the career of one of the most accomplished and desperate thieves that ever lived in Manchester was brought to an end,' he would later say.

There was also contentment in his private life. After living the life of a bachelor for almost half his life, Caminada married Amelia Wainhouse at the Holy Name church on Oxford Road at the age of thirty-seven. Living in nearby Chorlton-on-Medlock, the couple had three babies in just over two years, all of whom died before they were four months old. Eventually, they had a son who survived and prospered, but the personal pain Caminada suffered with the loss of the infants was inflicted tenfold on Manchester's underworld.

With a network of informers regularly meeting him at the 'Hidden Gem', nobody, it seemed, could slip under his radar. His reward was promotion to the position of detective superintendent, Manchester's first. Yet despite his success, he never rested on his laurels and in fact his most celebrated case was yet to come.

*

When Jerome Caminada was presented with the death of a wealthy businessman in mysterious circumstances, there were only a few scraps of information to work with. In fact, there was hardly any evidence supporting the theory that foul play had taken place. But Caminada's gut feeling was that he was dealing with a murder, and, piece by piece, he began to reconstruct the events of 26 February 1889.

The victim in question was John Fletcher, aged fifty, a wealthy Manchester paper manufacturer with a penchant for heavy drinking sessions with his cronies. It was on one such binge that he met up with a younger man whom it is believed he vaguely knew. With a hired 'growler' – the nickname for the driver of a four-wheeled, horse-drawn carriage – to ferry them around the city, the pair went on a bender that would end in tragedy.

As the cabman, Henry Goulding, drove them from one pub to another, he had a feeling that something untoward was about to happen and while travelling to an address in Hulme, his worst fears were realised. He was no more than halfway to the destination when crowds of people watching a circus parade brought the carriage to a virtual standstill. When a path cleared, Goulding attempted to make up for lost time, but was forced to pull over when a shout came from a passing pedestrian that a door was open at the side of his cab. It was not uncommon for people to do a runner, but nonetheless Goulding was surprised because one of his passengers had seemed well to do.

He looked back to see the younger of the two men sprinting away into the night, before he was lost to the shadows. Shaking his head, he got down to close the door, convinced he would be met with an empty carriage. But a puzzling sight greeted him: the older man, John Fletcher, was slumped, barely conscious, in the corner. Goulding, eager to get his fare, shook Fletcher to try and rouse him. It did not have the desired effect: after telling the cabbie to leave him alone, Fletcher lost consciousness and Goulding decided to enlist the help of the police to settle the matter.

A policeman, constable Jackman, was on his beat nearby and was summoned to the scene. He also tried to get some sense out of Fletcher, but after a few moments in the cab, he became concerned that Fletcher was more than just the worse for drink. In fact, his condition appeared to be rapidly deteriorating. The officer suggested that Goulding should head for Manchester Royal Infirmary and not spare the horses, which he did. On arrival, the two men lifted Fletcher out of the cab and heaved him towards the hospital entrance.

Before they could get him inside, Fletcher inhaled deeply, let out a sigh and died in their arms.

On the face of it, there was no sign that anything untoward had happened: the old boy had endured one drinking session too many and that was the sum and substance of it. Caminada, however, instinctively smelled a rat and began carefully to piece together what had happened.

Fletcher was positively identified by a Manchester and Southport Bank cheque book found in his jacket pocket. With his identity established, Caminada needed to know who the victim was and what sort of character he was. Gradually, a picture emerged. Fletcher worked in Manchester and on the day of his death had attended the sale of a mill at the Mitre Hotel shortly after lunch but his movements after that were unknown.

The businessman, who lived in Southport some fifty miles from Manchester, was a well-known figure in the public houses of the city centre. Caminada surmised his weakness for alcohol might have made him an easy target for opportunistic criminals. He also needed to know why Fletcher's young companion had been keen to get away in such a hurry and also where the pair had been intending to go on the fateful journey.

Fletcher's nephew said that his uncle had been wearing gold-rimmed spectacles and an expensive gold watch and was carrying a substantial amount of cash when he last saw him. Caminada was already aware that, but for a few pennies, no cash or valuables were discovered on the deceased's person. The gold pocket watch he always carried would have certainly attracted the wrong kind of attention: it was worth £120, twice the yearly earnings of the average working man. To the shrewd detective, it seemed highly likely that he was dealing with a robbery gone wrong.

Having established a motive and identified a chief suspect, Caminada now needed to find the man who had fled the cab. The trail was hotting up, but it would prove anything but straightforward. Caminada first ruled out the address the men had been heading to: 43 Stretford Road, Hulme, which was nothing more than a lock-up tailor's shop whose owner knew neither Fletcher nor his drinking companion. The detective concluded it was a bogus destination. Caminada then interviewed several witnesses at the Mitre Hotel which in turn led him to Sinclair's Oyster Rooms, where Fletcher had said he was heading for a meal. Close to Sinclair's was a dried-fish-and-game stall and when Caminada questioned its owner, Edward Lait, he got his first real break. Lait recalled seeing Fletcher chatting with a younger man around six o'clock that evening, and another witness stated that he too had seen the deceased, wearing his distinctive pocket watch and glasses.

A landlady at one of the pubs the cabbie had later taken them to on their city-centre pub crawl – the notorious Three Arrows – recalled serving the men, though she couldn't add much more. By retracing the final route of the cab, Caminada figured the murderer may have gone into the nearest pub after fleeing the scene to lie low for a short time. If that was the case, he would have plenty of cash on his person and possibly a gold watch. Surely someone would have remembered him.

The York Minster was the closest pub and it turned out that Caminada's hunch was right on the money. Landlord Andrew Holt confirmed a young man had called in on the night in question and ordered milk and a soda before getting in a cab. Crucially, he had stayed in the landlord's mind – and that of several other members of staff – because of the expensive watch he had pulled out of his jacket to check the time. He was also carrying a large amount of money, judging by the wad of notes he had on him. Caminada reasoned that his quarry might be crafty, but his behaviour after the crime was sloppy. Did he have the confidence of a man who had got away with similar offences in the past?

Caminada had little difficulty tracing the cabbie. William Coleman had taken the young man on from the York Minster after agreeing a fee of 1s 7d for the journey to the Locomotive Inn on Oldham Road. That pub was known locally as Jack Rooks, and was a well-known haunt of bare-knuckle boxers and assorted hard men. Caminada knew the premises, and the landlord, John Parton, well. He figured the fugitive – for whom he now had a decent description thanks to numerous witnesses – was probably a pugilist. There would have been no other reason to brave the menacing atmosphere of Jack Rooks unless, of course, he was either a member of the landlord's family, or a close friend.

John Parton was thought to be involved in a range of criminal activities although nothing was ever proven. It was of great interest to Caminada that Parton had long been suspected by numerous inform-ants of spiking mouthwash used by opponents of boxers he had backed. While he didn't fit the physical description of the wanted man, perhaps one of his sons would. A succession of young men who frequented Jack Rooks were interviewed; to a man they were gnarly faced with the obligatory cauliflower ears and misshapen noses. While no one directly pointed an accusing finger, the names 'Pig Jack or 'Pig Jack's son', cropped up time and again.

Pig Jack was John Parton's nickname and he had also been the landlord of a pub in Salford where his beer was renowned for hitting the spot within a couple of pints, too accurately in fact. Jelly-legged and dizzy, punters would stagger out and collapse, only to awaken to sore heads and considerably lighter wallets. Pig Jack drugged their beer and then lightened their load, but since most his of his customers were thieves anyway, the crimes went unreported and were difficult for victims to prove.

As Parton had grown more confident in his ability to drug victims, he began to fix boxing matches, spiking mouthwash and waging hefty sums on the bout's outcome. Even in the criminal world, Pig Jack was playing a dangerous game and one he would undoubtedly pay for with his life should the truth come to light. One of his sons, Charles, an amateur boxer, fitted the description of John Fletcher's drinking associate perfectly and Caminada reasoned there was a strong probability he had inherited his father's pharmaceutical skills. If so, the jigsaw was falling neatly into place.

Charles Parton, a stocky 18-year-old, denied any knowledge of John Fletcher. He claimed to have been in Liverpool on the day of Fletcher's death and said he had not returned to Manchester until six in the evening, spending the rest of the night at home. Caminada, however, was convinced after the first interview that he had his man and following a thorough search of Parton's lodgings, discovered two gold sovereigns and pair of gold-rimmed spectacles underneath his bed. Charles Parton was arrested and following several identity parades, witnesses confirmed him as the man who was with Fletcher on the night of his death. But while a motive was clear, there was no evidence that Parton had contributed to Fletcher's death. The case lacked a 'smoking gun'.

Then came the breakthrough Caminada needed to turn his hunch into a conviction. He recalled that while sifting through a pile of routine reports, there had been a curious theft in Liverpool. He located the file and read with interest that a young man in his late teens had attempted to purchase forty grains of chloral, a hypnotic and anaesthetic hydrate, which he said was for his aunt's heart condition. He had no prescription, so his request was refused but after the man pleaded that the situation was urgent, the chemist agreed to sell him ten grains. As he carefully made up the order, the customer reached over, snatched the bottle and fled. Could this have been Parton? Caminada suspected he was involved in some form of doping, given his father's background. If the chemist could make a formal identification and a post-mortem confirmed traces of the same compound, he would have his smoking gun – and enough proof to ensure a murder conviction.

To Caminada's relief, the Liverpudlian chemist identified the thief as Charles Parton and Fletcher's body did indeed show traces of chloral in his internal organs. For Parton, the game was up, though whether he had intended to kill John Fletcher, or had just tried to knock him out, remained in doubt. When the story was reported in the papers, two more victims came forward and said they too had been drugged and robbed by Parton. It was the final nail in the youngster's coffin and at his trial in St George's Hall, Liverpool a jury took just twenty minutes to convict him of murder, but with a strong recommendation for mercy.

Parton was sentenced to death by the judge, Mr Justice Charles, but spared hanging just four days before the execution was due to take place. It had been his rotten luck that Jerome Caminada was in charge of his case, one that could easily have been passed off as little more than robbery and death by natural causes in the hands of lesser mortals. It is interesting to note that one of the victims of Parton's previous chemically assisted crimes died shortly after the murderer's reprieve, from the effects of being drugged.

*

In 1899, Manchester's criminal fraternity breathed a collective sigh of relief when Jerome Caminada retired. He had been responsible for imprisoning an astonishing 1,125 men and women during his time with the force and he was given a substantial pension as a reward. In 1901 he published his memoirs *Twenty-Five Years of Detective Life* and tried his hand at being a private detective, estate agent and, briefly, a local councillor, for Openshaw. After years of tackling some of the most notorious criminals in one of Europe's toughest cities and surviving several attempts on his life, it is perhaps ironic that it was a bus – and not a gun-toting crook out for vengeance – that finally got the better of him. In March 1914, he was hit by the vehicle while in North Wales and died at his home in Moss Side as a result of his injuries several months later, aged seventy.

There were many tributes to him, including one from Judge Parry, who had known him professionally for thirty years. Parry described Caminada as a 'genius', stating that he 'knew criminals and their ways as a zoologist knows the lower animals'. Caminada, the judge concluded, 'was the Garibaldi of detectives'. Being compared to the great hero of Italy would have been gratifying for Jerome Caminada, who was very proud of his Italian heritage.

His body was buried in Southern Cemetery and his grave is maintained by former members of Greater Manchester Police, who, in

1984, formed the Caminada Society which, incidentally, is still going strong today with around three hundred members.

A fitting epitaph for a man who was – and remains – Manchester's greatest detective.

11

UNITED CITY: MANCHESTER AFTER MUNICH

This is a numbing tragedy. It stuns the mind to try to grasp that the flower of English football has fallen. It is a tragedy that will be felt not only by sports-lovers but by all the people of Manchester and indeed by many others all over the world.

Manchester Evening News editorial, 7 February 1958

The story is so well known. Not just to Mancunians and football fans, but also to people the world over. The Munich Disaster of 6 February 1958, which caused the deaths of twenty-three passengers and crew, including eight Manchester United players, is the most-talked about aviation accident in history. The fabled Busby Babes, nurtured so lovingly by a legendary manager, were cruelly cut down in the prime of their football lives. That the club recovered and enjoyed a golden age in the 1960s is little short of miraculous. It is a story that has been told so often and so eloquently and with every anniversary of Munich it is told again. And rightly so.

The charter plane – an Elizabethan-class Airspeed Ambassador called Lord Burghley and operated by British European Airways – was flying back to Manchester from Belgrade and had stopped at Munich-Riem airport to refuel. On board was the Manchester United team that had just qualified for the last four of the European Cup, thanks to a second-leg 3–3 draw against Red Star Belgrade, which followed a 2–1 win at Old Trafford. It was a bitterly cold afternoon, with heavy snow on the runway, hardly ideal for flying. What made matters worse was that the plane had been experiencing significant engine problems, resulting in James Thain, the captain, aborting two attempts at takeoff. However, at just after three o'clock, Thain made a third attempt to get flight 609 airborne. This time it was fatal: the plane ran into slush at the end of the runway, careered out of control and crashed through a fence before hitting a house, the port wing ripping off in the process.

Despite the heroics of Harry Gregg, the team's goalkeeper, who helped to pull survivors from the hulk, seven of the Busby Babes died instantly: Geoff Bent, Roger Byrne, Eddie Colman, Mark Jones, David Pegg, Tommy Taylor and Liam Whelan. Others, very seriously injured, were rushed to the local Rechts der Isar hospital, among them Jackie Blanchflower, Johnny Berry, Dennis Viollet, Albert Scanlon and Duncan Edwards. Matt Busby was also seriously hurt in the collision and he too was rushed to Rechts der Isar. A number of the club's backroom staff were also killed, along with eight journalists who had been travelling with the United party. The newspapermen included Frank Swift, one of Manchester City's greatest-ever goalkeepers, but who now made his living from reporting on the sport he had graced. Although co-pilot Ken Rayment later died of his injuries, James Thain survived.

Perhaps inevitably, the story of Munich tends to focus on the most famous and most talented. On Duncan Edwards, the powerhouse wing half destined to become England's greatest ever player, on Bobby Charlton, an extravagantly gifted inside forward who would win 106 caps for his country and inspire England to the 1966 World Cup, on Matt Busby the managerial genius who transformed the fortunes of Manchester United after the Second World War. The story, equally inevitably, always explains how this great institution rose from the ashes and regained its rightful place in the pantheon of world football.

Yet there is an important facet of the Munich tale that does not receive so much attention. How did the people of Manchester react to what happened on that fateful day? How did United's greatest rivals, Manchester City, and their fans, respond to the tragedy? How did official Manchester, the Manchester of town hall, churches and businesses react? Munich, inevitably, touched everyone in this great city. It is time to tell their story.

The first inkling that something tragic had occurred came at Old Trafford. Manchester United fans had gone to their beloved stadium to buy tickets for an FA Cup tie with Sheffield Wednesday but when the news began to filter in from Germany the sale was suspended. Most of the fans hung around, anxious for more news. Within hours, as the full shocking details were hammered out on teleprinters, the whole city had heard about the crash and the fatalities. It was too much to bear. The grief was uncontrollable, as the *Manchester Evening Chronicle* reported.

> Manchester was a city of sorrow today. The man-in-the-street was still numb with shock from the news . . . . Men wore black ties as a mark of respect. . . . Many of the women interviewed this morning fought back tears as they spoke of the tragedy.

Individual Manchester United fans were bereft, feeling a deep sense of personal loss. John Quinn, a plumber from Campbell Road in Longsight, and a Red for thirty-six years, summed it up well: 'When you have followed a team all that time and shared in their successes and defeats, when disaster strikes them it becomes a personal loss. I knew some of the players quite well.'

Quinn was not the only fan who would have known the players well. The stars of the 1950s lived in the same neighbourhoods as the fans; they were not isolated from the people who followed them, not like the players of today with their vast salaries and mansions on gated estates. To keep fit and to have fun they even used the facilities at a place that no modern-day player would ever dream of patronising: the YMCA. In his message of condolence R. F. Torrington, secretary of the Manchester YMCA, observed that the entire United squad were members of the organisation and used the gym and swimming pool every week. In the days before foreign imports dominated our game a high proportion of the players were local lads. The likes of Byrne, Bent, Colman, Scanlon and Viollet hailed from the Manchester area; they were not just for the people, but of the people, and that made the emotional connection so much stronger.

Without a moment's hesitation the fans and officials of Manchester City set aside the great rivalry with their local neighbours. The City chairman, Alan Douglas, spoke from the heart.

> I am very upset by this tragedy. I knew many of the party personally and I express my deep sympathy to the relatives of those who may have

died. . . . We are very, very sorry for the United club. If there is any help we can give to them we shall.

City's keeper, the great Bert Trautmann – a man with first-hand know-ledge of death and destruction on a huge scale thanks to his wartime service on the Russian Front – weighed in with a heartfelt article for the *Evening News*.

> I still find it hard to believe that these men whose hands I'd held in friendship so long won't be here anymore. We all feel that way about it at Maine Road. It has struck us very hard because although we were possibly United's strongest rivals, we were also neighbours, which means friends.

His sentiments were echoed by City captain, Dave Ewing: 'Anything we can do to help in any way we shall do with all our hearts.' They were replicated by fans of a light-blue persuasion. The *Chronicle* noted that the wave of sympathy engulfing the city stemmed also from the 'other place: Maine Road'. Les Harrup, (35) of Alpine Street, Clayton, and a City supporter, told the paper 'It is a great tragedy and I sympathise with all those who are left behind.'

Civic Manchester also responded magnificently. Lord Mayor Leslie (later Sir Leslie) Lever, recognising the impact the disaster had had around the world, immediately set up the Manchester United Disaster Fund. The objective was to remember those who had perished by the erection of a monument. 'I have never known in the whole of my life public opinion so stirred and I am sure that all sections of the city, the country and the world will be anxious to join in the establishment of such a worthy memorial,' he explained.

Within hours, the fund had received its first donation, of 1,000 guineas, from Great Universal Stores. Other businesses were quick to contribute: the *Manchester Evening News* and the *Manchester Guardian* contributed £1,000 as did the *Manchester Evening Chronicle*. The Pools Promoters' Association, made up of Littlewoods, Vernon's, Copes and Murphy's, gave a thousand guineas. Harry Vos, a gown maker of Spear Street, donated £100. Manchester City would also play its part: before the home game with Birmingham City the club allowed a special collection to be taken for the Disaster Fund.

The Lord Mayor had his work cut out. Leslie Lever was up all night taking messages of sympathy: not only from Britain but also from towns and cities all over the world. Pope Pius XII sent his condolences while President of Tito of Yugoslavia, in whose country the match had taken place, did likewise. But Lever was particularly gratified to receive the following statement from Her Majesty the Queen.

> I am deeply shocked to hear of the accident to the plane carrying members of Manchester United FC and newspapermen coming back from Belgrade. Please convey my sympathy and that of my husband to the relatives of those who have been killed and to the injured.

In the House of Commons, Minister of Transport Harold Watkinson was heard in 'solemn silence' as he gave a full account of the crash. He expressed his deepest sympathy for the relatives of the deceased and the 'unusually large numbers of MPs present' murmured their approval. While, from across the world, football associations sent telegrams to the FA expressing their sorrow at what had happened.

Other local figures played their part. In Urmston, where many of the United players lived, chairman councillor Albert Williams called on Mrs Joy Byrne, wife of Roger, who was now a widow at the age of just twenty-three. She and Roger had moved into a new house in the area just seven months previously, after their wedding in St Mary's, Droylsden. Councillor Williams went on to visit the homes of Ray Wood, Johnny Berry and Dennis Viollet, expressing the sympathy of the town to the bereaved and to those families with injured loved ones.

On the first Saturday night after the disaster the mood was very different from normal. Manchester is invariably vibrant, full of the joys of spring, at the weekend. This time it was different. At the Plaza ballroom, manager 'Jim' Savile (yes *that* Jimmy Savile, but for once he would do the right thing) was hosting the annual dance for the staff of Walkers Showcards. He stopped the dancing and asked revellers to donate money to the Lord Mayor's Disaster Fund for as long as he could hold his breath. While Savile was doing his best not to inhale, the Walkers staff showered copper, silver and notes onto the floor in 'a tinkling cascade'. Over at the Midland Hotel the members of Stockport's Bramall Park golf club had a two-minute silence before their annual dinner dance. These scenes were repeated in pubs and clubs across the city that night.

On the Sunday morning, church congregations across Britain prayed for the dead and the injured, nowhere more fervently than in Manchester. In Matt Busby's church of St John's Chorlton-cum-Hardy his mother, brother, sister and aunt shared their grief and anxiety with hundreds of churchgoers. A few miles away, at the church of St Peter, Stretford, in which parish Old Trafford is located, children sang a special anthem.

Yet the greatest outpouring of emotion was still to come. On the Monday after the crash a plane touched down at Ringway airport. In the hold were seventeen coffins. The reality of what had happened in Munich now hit the people of Manchester like a hammer.

The scenes at the airport were heartbreaking. Five hundred people were crowded into the public enclosure: club officials, civic dignitaries, among them Lord Mayor Lever, and a host of ordinary fans, 'many of them young boys muffled up against the cold with their red-and-white United scarves'. The plane landed two hours late and baggage handlers quickly lifted dozens of wreaths – some of them six feet in diameter – from the hold. Then came the sight that those present would never forget. Slowly, and with infinite care, seventeen coffins were lifted off the plane and eased into seventeen black hearses.

The great procession of hearses drove slowly out of the airport. Its destination was Old Trafford and it was now that the people of the city, putting historic rivalries aside, came together as one.

They did Manchester proud that day.

Estimates of the numbers who lined the eleven-mile route start at one hundred thousand. In reality there were many more but that does not matter. What matters is the respectful and dignified behaviour of those present, who came from all walks of life. 'Businessmen in their new cars . . . Teddy Boys . . . . housewives carrying young children, cloth-capped men with cycles, schoolboys, office girls in headscarves,' as the *Evening News* observes.

They had been there for hours, waiting to pay their respects. On a cold, moonless, starlit night the mourners, in places ten deep, stood shoulder-to-shoulder, then huddled together for shelter as the rain came. So great were the crowds that in places there was barely enough room for the cortège to pass. Never before had Manchester witnessed such scenes of mass grief and devotion.

It is often said that the English were emotionally liberated after the passing of Diana, Princess of Wales in 1997. That the huge outpouring of grief occasioned by her death led to the loosening of the stiff upper lip for which this nation was once renowned. Before Diana, they say, we were reluctant to show our feelings in public, even at the funeral of a loved one.

They should have been in Manchester on that winter's night in February 1958.

One journalist noted that as the hearses passed 'women wearing headscarves and heavy coats with upturned collars wept unashamedly'. In Chorlton 'a small group of men knelt on the pavement in prayer'. These scenes were repeated all along that vale of tears. Interviews with individual mourners capture the mood well. A Teddy Boy wearing tight blue jeans nodded to his girlfriend and said, 'I'm a City fan really but she's a United fan. She cried her heart out when she heard.'

At Old Trafford there were five thousand gathered on the surrounding streets, patiently waiting for the hearses carrying their heroes. For miles on end the roads were lined with cars parked nose-to-tail. As the cortège passed, 'The full-throated roar of a motorcycle engine cut like a knife through the strangely still air.' Then as the massed ranks of mourners – some weeping, others praying, yet others silent but sombre – looked on as the coffins were removed from their hearses and taken up to the stadium gym. In the gym, which was festooned with flowers, each coffin was draped in black and placed carefully on its own table.

The next morning there were still more incredible scenes. Before dawn workers heading for Trafford Park stopped off at the ground, standing heads bowed outside the main entrance, which was the closest point to the gym. Their devotion prompted a groundsman to observe that, 'It has been a remarkable sight, seeing men on bikes and on foot paying homage.' A policeman stood guard outside, surrounded by a sea of wreaths. No one was allowed into the gym despite the club being inundated with phone calls from fans asking if they could get in to pay their respects.

Letters poured into the newspapers from people in the Manchester area and from India, Canada, Australia, Ireland, the United States, all four corners of the globe in fact. Many exiled Mancunians wrote to express their sorrow, a significant number of them enclosing donations for the Lord Mayor's Disaster Fund. The *Manchester Evening News* published a letter from a Salford man, H. C. Whitehead of Welford Street, which summed up the feelings of thousands: 'United belong to Manchester and Manchester is united as never before. The sun will shine later on.'

Sadly, the grief experienced by one man pushed him over the edge. John Bunn of Northwich stabbed himself to death with a Scout knife after becoming depressed about Munich. The coroner recorded that Mr Bunn had killed himself while, 'The balance of his mind was disturbed.'

As the days passed, the focus switched to those lying in German sickbeds. They were being well cared for. BEA, the flight operators, spared no expense, paying a huge amount of money to secure the services of the best doctors. No less than five surgeons attended to Busby and the treatment afforded to his players was also first class. The people of Munich opened their hearts to the United group being treated in their hospital, flooding the wards with flowers and sweets. American GIs, stationed in the city, were also very kind and sent comics, magazines and books, much appreciated because they were in English.

Back home, the desire for news was overwhelming. In the days before the internet and twenty-four-hours-a-day television channels, there was a heavy reliance on the newspapers. They did their best to satisfy readers, with bulletins being published every day in the local press. This one from the *Chronicle* is fairly representative:

Busby: Critical
Edwards: Serious
Blanchflower: Satisfactory
Taylor: Serious
Morgans: Good
Scanlon: Quite Good
Charlton: Good

While there was rejoicing when the likes of Bobby Charlton, Harry Gregg and Bill Foulkes were able to leave Munich and make the long journey home, people waited anxiously for updates on those still receiving treatment, especially Matt Busby and Duncan Edwards.

The manager's condition was very serious, so serious in fact that he was twice given the last rites in hospital. Given the nature of his injuries a decision had been made to spare him the devastating effect the crash had wreaked on his young team. When Jimmy Murphy called to see him in hospital a doctor discreetly took the Old Trafford assistant manager aside and whispered in his ear: 'He does not realise any of them are gone. You must not tell him.'

Then, as Murphy stooped low over the bed, Busby, smiling faintly despite the pain that racked his body, uttered the most poignant statement his loyal number two had ever heard: 'If this thing had to happen thank goodness I was the one who was knocked about.'

It was typical of the man.

Inevitably, the papers wrote hundreds of column inches on the biggest star of them all: Duncan Edwards. Right from the start Edwards was described as 'dangerously ill'. His injuries were terrible: broken ribs, severely damaged kidneys, a collapsed lung, a broken pelvis and a complete fracture of the right thigh. Despite this doctors were optimistic that he could pull through. He was a perfect physical specimen, as strong as an ox.

It soon became clear that their optimism was misplaced. Duncan Edwards continued to deteriorate. Desperate times call for desperate measures and an artificial kidney was rushed in a police car from a clinic at Freiburg University, two hundred miles away. When it was fitted he showed definite signs of improvement. The device had taken the strain off his injured kidneys and they were now functioning normally. Doctors expressed their amazement at his powers of recovery. He even regained consciousness, sat up and murmured, 'Where am I?' Then, for a few seconds, he thought he was playing football and shouted 'Goal, goal!'

Back in Manchester, as England's greatest player fought for his life, the people of Manchester began the grim task of burying the dead. Roger Byrne, the United captain, had his funeral at St Michael's, Flixton, which was packed to the rafters with mourners, including many dignitaries, while five hundred more stood silently outside. The service for little Eddie Colman – a local lad from Archie Street in Salford and a favourite of the Old Trafford crowd – was equally poignant; thousands lined the streets along Regent New Road and Eccles New Road to watch the cortège leave the church, where the congregation had included Lord Mayor Leslie Lever and Jimmy Murphy. It was not only in Manchester that big crowds turned out: Tommy Taylor, a prolific goal scorer for both his club and England, was laid to rest in his native Barnsley and police struggled to marshal the huge numbers who had gathered around the church to bid farewell to a fellow Tyke.

The sad litany of funerals continued. At St John's Pendlebury three thousand were present to say goodbye to reserve left back Geoff Bent, where the mourners included Dave Ewing. David Pegg, a son of Yorkshire, was buried in Doncaster; Irishman Billy Whelan in Dublin. That gentle giant of a man Frank Swift, a hero to Manchester City fans, went to his final resting place after a moving ceremony in St Margaret's, Whalley Range; there was not a seat to be had inside and three hundred stood outside in the winter sunshine among fifty wreaths.

The emotion-filled services for the young footballers were matched by those held to honour the journalists who had perished. Men like Tom Jackson of the *Manchester Evening News*. Jackson travelled thousands of miles at home and abroad to report on United. He was a personal friend and maybe something of a father figure to the players, giving them advice and helping them to solve little problems. The Old Trafford fans trusted him; they knew he was Manchester United through and through. He had arrived at the *News* straight from school at the tender age of fourteen, initially as a rather chubby messenger boy. However, he was determined to become a reporter and he later achieved his ambition, at first on the crime desk and then, after war service and to his great joy, as the 'United' man on the paper. His colleagues paid him a generous tribute, mounting a plaque behind his desk on the newsroom wall. It read simply: 'Tom Jackson, Master Reporter'.

The death of Jackson's fellow reporter, Alf Clarke of the *Manchester Evening Chronicle*, must have been hard to take for his family, given the events that preceded it. After the second unsuccessful takeoff the passengers had gone back to the departure lounge. Clarke then telephoned his news desk and, engrossed in the call, missed the announcement about getting back on board. As the crew grew impatient the plane nearly took off without him but somehow he managed to take his seat, dying instantly in the crash. Alf Clarke, like Tom Jackson, would receive many heartfelt tributes from journalists and readers.

Only one reporter of the nine who had been on board the Elizabethan survived. He was even able to read, in his own paper, that he had perished in Munich. Frank Taylor, attached to the *News Chronicle*, was seriously injured and hospitalised for five months. But he recovered, despite the *Chronicle* publishing his obituary. To paraphrase Mark Twain, whose passing was also prematurely reported, 'rumours of my death have been greatly exaggerated'.

Then there came the news that every Manchester United fan – indeed everyone in England – had been dreading. Duncan Edwards was dead. The medical team in Germany, noting his superhuman will to live, had dared to hope that his courage would pull him through. It was not to be. At quarter past two on the morning of 21 February 1958, he passed away. The cause of death was kidney failure; those vital organs could function no longer. Only some of his teammates in the hospital were told – Dennis Viollet, Ray Wood, Ken Morgans and Albert Scanlon, all of whom survived Munich – and they wept bitterly when given the news. The others – Johnny Berry, Jackie Blanchflower and Busby – were simply too ill to be disturbed, although all three men would made it back to England.

The tributes paid to Edwards were, of course, fulsome, even adulatory. That was hardly surprising as many who had played with and against him considered that the man from Dudley in the West Midlands was the greatest player they had ever seen. A debutant for Manchester United at just sixteen, and a full international with England at eighteen, there seemed no limit to his potential. Not known for hyperbole, Bobby Charlton remarked that, 'Compared to him the rest of us are like pygmies.' The blue side of the city was also quick to eulogise the man and former Maine Road captain Roy Paul said it was, 'One of the greatest tragedies of soccer. Here was a boy who was by far the greatest half-back I've ever seen – and he was not yet at his peak. His death is a blow English soccer will feel for years.'

The only city that came close to feeling the sadness experienced in Manchester was one located a thousand miles to the east: Belgrade, where the European Cup quarter-final between United and Red Star had been staged. The two clubs, their players and backroom staff had got on like a house on fire from the outset, despite the on-field rivalry. All 55,000 tickets for the second leg in Yugoslavia had been sold and the game itself was exciting; hard-fought, yet always sporting.

After the match both teams attended a banquet, at which Matt Busby gave a short speech, in which he emphasised the bonds of friendship that had developed between the two clubs. 'There were many surprises for me in the second half of the match and the most pleasant surprise of all is the close friendship of all of us here. I do hope we meet more often . . .'

No doubt gratified that they had reached the semi-final of the European Cup, Busby allowed his young charges to go out on the town after the banquet. The United players were accompanied by a party of Yugoslav players and journalists, and the carousing ended with a visit to a night club. In the course of the evening, thanks to the universal language that is football, friendships were forged and plans made to keep in touch. Tommy Taylor and Sekularac, a young Red Star player, really hit it off and each invited the other for a holiday in their respective countries. Later, when the Yugoslav found out that Taylor had died he wept like a child.

> I feel unhappy and depressed as never before in my life. When we parted Taylor said to me 'So long until May when we will meet in the World Cup in Stockholm and afterwards for our holidays in Dalmatia.' This horrible death has broken my heart, but I will always keep in my heart the remembrance of my good and great Taylor.

It was not just Sekularac who was affected by Munich. In a report for the *Manchester Evening News*, Yugoslav journalist Vinko Sale describes the wave of emotion the tragedy unleashed in his native Belgrade.

> At first nobody believed it. But later huge crowds of soccer fans came out on the street. They gathered in front of the radio station and news agencies to hear the latest news of the tragic crash. I feel specially grieved. I welcomed the team and I saw them off at the airport. I have made friends with all of them but death has broken those friendships.

Manchester was not yet done. More than two weeks after the disaster it was still fresh in the mind. That is why on 24 February 1958 an astonishing six thousand people attended mass for the fallen at King's Hall, Belle Vue. The Bishop of Salford presided, and was assisted by a phalanx of priests and eighty-five choirboys from St Bede's College in Alexandra Park. In the congregation there were a large number of civic dignitaries. During the service Canon William Sewell, from Matt Busby's parish church of St John's, told the huge assembly of Billy Whelan's last words on the plane: 'This may be death. I'm ready. We should all be ready every day for this crisis.' The Church of England also organised a memorial service. At Manchester Cathedral more than fifteen hundred mourners filled the ancient building. 'Never in its 1,000-year history has the cathedral seen such a remarkable congregation for a service,' pronounced the dean, the Very Reverend H. A. Jones.

On the field United, of course, would rise again and reach even greater heights. Despite suffering the most grievous blow of any team in the history of the game there was a grim determination to carry on. The agenda was clearly laid out by United chairman Harold Hardman, just twenty-four hours after the accident. Hardman insisted that the club would carry on with their full league, FA Cup and European Cup programme, even if it meant heavy defeats. 'We have a duty to the public and a duty to football,' he announced.

In Busby's absence Jimmy Murphy kept things going in the immediate aftermath, putting out what was virtually a scratch team for the first game after the tragedy, an FA Cup tie, at home, against Sheffield Wednesday. The demand for tickets was unprecedented and the inevitable black market pushed prices to astronomical levels, with United fans desperate to back their team in its hour of need. Before the game, telegrams flooded in from all over the world, offering their best wishes. One however stood out from all the rest: it was sent by the widow of club secretary Walter Crickmer, who had perished at Munich. It read: 'Whatever happens, keep the United flag flying.'

In the tie with Wednesday the Reds were unstoppable, winning comfortably by three goals to nil. Despite having to field a much-weakened side for the rest of the season, the 1958 FA Cup final was reached; sadly, however, the game was lost by two goals to nil. In due course Matt Busby would return and guide the team to many more triumphs, a run that culminated in Manchester United becoming the first English team to win the European Cup in 1968.

While the formal mourning might have concluded with those two huge set-piece occasions at Belle Vue and Manchester Cathedral, the good people of Manchester have never forgotten the dead of Munich. And they never will. In the dark days of February 1958 red and blue came together in a spirit of togetherness because it was Manchester's loss. For that reason it is fitting that the last word should go to a City fan, who summed up how everyone felt.

> On behalf of thousands of City supporters, our deepest sympathy in the air disaster that overtook 'Our Pride of the World – Manchester United.' We send deepest sympathy to the bereaved families of those footballers, officials and sports writers who lost their lives.

> Just Blue

12

AN ACT OF FAITH: THE MANCHESTER SHIP CANAL

The first of January 1894 was a cause for celebration in Manchester. And not just because it was New Year's Day. Something special was happening, something way out of the ordinary; something that everyone in the city wanted to be part of. The opening to traffic of the Manchester Ship Canal. Seven years in the making and twelve in the planning, it was a triumph of commercial and engineering expertise. It is doubtful if any other city in Britain, save perhaps London, would have had the capacity to complete such a gargantuan undertaking.

The statistics are staggering. Stretching thirty-five miles from Eastham on the Mersey estuary to the Pomona docks, the ship canal made Manchester, an inland city, a great port, one of the biggest in Britain. It had been dug to the same depth as the Suez Canal (26 feet), but at 120 feet was wider even than that great waterway. The very latest machinery was used in the construction process, including 75 steam excavators, 124 steam cranes and 7 earth dredgers. Some of the technological feats were, for the time, spectacular, including the triple entrance locks and the Barton Aqueduct, which carried the Bridgewater Canal over the new waterway.

It is little wonder that one local paper of the time, the *Manchester City News* (and, incidentally, the only press outlet to support the project from its inception) was inspired to describe it as 'the grandest undertaking ever realised in this country, and a permanent memorial of what may be justly described as the greatest non-martial triumph that has ever been witnessed'. The writer had perhaps got a little carried away, but not by much. It had been a herculean challenge, expertly delivered. And let us not forget the human input: the numbers employed ran into the tens of thousands, making it the biggest private-sector employer in Europe.

It may well be asked why such a project was necessary in the first place. To make a city so far from the open sea into a major port seems to go against the laws not just of geography but also of economics. Surely, a better, and cheaper, solution could have been found. To discover why Manchester embarked on such an enterprise we must look at its place in the world.

By the middle of the nineteenth century, Manchester had become the greatest industrial city on the planet, the legendary Cottonopolis, a place where ambition and thinking big was in the DNA of its buccaneering businessmen. Thanks largely to the growth of the textile industries, and in particular cotton processing, its rise had been nothing short of spectacular. From a middling town of 27,000 people in the 1770s, Manchester had grown to 137,000 by 1811 and to nearly 200,000 by the 1850s. Success on that scale breeds self-assurance, the sense that no challenge is too big to be tackled.

Such was the self-confidence of its leading citizens that the city often thought the unthinkable. In 1894 the *Manchester Guardian* – the region's imperious and highly influential newspaper – argued, quite seriously, that Manchester would make a better capital city than London: 'It occupies, in point of fact, the exact centre of modern industrial and commercial Britain . . . London is a southern suburb of Lancashire and Yorkshire.' That, alas, was a step too far even for Victorian Manchester, which nevertheless continued to scale new heights of commercial success.

There was, however, one rather troublesome fly in the ointment. Manchester businesses felt they were being held back by two factors, both of which were outwith their control: the charges imposed on freight by the port of Liverpool and the excessive prices demanded by railway companies to take goods to and from Merseyside. The city's prosperity was being affected and many felt that something had to be done. There were those in Manchester who believed it would be enough to renegotiate terms with Liverpool and the railways. Others however, more ambitious and visionary, argued that a much bolder solution was needed.

The idea of a canal was first mooted as far back as 1714 when Thomas Steers, a Manchester businessman, and others, formed the Mersey and Irwell Navigation Company but at that time the technical and political challenges were just too difficult to overcome. By 1824, with improved technology, and Manchester desperate for a more economical way to export its goods, the idea was back on the agenda. Once again a company was formed, but the many vested interests ranged against the project wasted no time in lobbying Parliament and the politicians of the day swiftly rejected the scheme. Manchester's misfortune gave some people a great deal of amusement: public figures in Liverpool, and that city's partisan press, had a field day while comedians had music-hall audiences hooting with laughter.

However, by the late 1870s the issue of creating a new link to the sea was again being hotly debated. The British economy, after a boom that had lasted for decades, was in a deep recession and Manchester had suffered, along with the rest of the country. The high freight charges imposed by the Mersey docks and the railway companies made things even worse, with one study calculating that of Liverpool's £4.5 million annual customs duty, two-thirds was paid by Manchester companies. One Manchester businessman spoke for many when he pointedly stated that Liverpool depended for its existence 'on the milk of Manchester from which it takes off the cream'.

Given that times were hard and money difficult to raise it perhaps wasn't the best time to be embarking on such a risky endeavour but Manchester had a powerful can-do attitude. The city was also fortunate that a doughty champion came to the fore at just the right time. His name was Daniel Adamson and if one man can be said to have been the driving force behind the new venture it was him. A successful entrepreneur – he was the owner of an engineering works in Dukinfield – Adamson was not one to stand idly by and let his beloved city go to rack and ruin. He issued a call to arms and seventy of the great and the good answered it. On 27 June 1882, they convened at his home – The Towers, in Didsbury – where he passionately made the case for the canal.

'If the Suez Canal, situated in a barbarous country . . . could be carried out there ought to be no engineering difficulties to stand in the way as far as the Mersey is concerned,' Adamson thundered. The assembled throng murmured its approval and after some discussion it was agreed that a feasibility study should be commissioned. Once again there was hostility to the plan, from, perhaps surprisingly, the *Manchester Guardian* and, more predictably, from the merchants of Liverpool. But this time there would be no going back. Not long after the meeting, the Manchester Ship Canal Company was set up.

When the feasibility study showed that the canal was economically viable, the company decided to press on. The first step was to get legal approval for the work and this would require much more than simple planning permission from the council. Because of the scale of the proposed project an Act of Parliament was required, which would of course mean persuading the politicians in Westminster. This was a tortuous process that took three years. During that time Adamson lobbied furiously for the canal, making speeches all over the north-west. He drew huge crowds, electrifying them with his 'eloquent, north-country style of speaking,' as one historian describes it. At a meeting in Manchester's Free Trade Hall that Adamson was to address such was the public's interest that two-thousand disappointed spectators had to be turned away. He also organised two huge petitions, one of which contained no less than two-hundred-thousand signatures and was so big that it needed six porters to carry it into the House of Commons.

The pressure brought to bear by Adamson and his supporters worked. Parliament passed the necessary legislation in late 1885 and the reaction in Manchester was little short of hysterical. A public holiday was declared in the city to allow the people to celebrate, and celebrate they did. A huge, enthusiastic crowd, numbering close to forty thousand, gathered in Albert Square. The joy among the people was clear as they marched with a spring in their step to Belle Vue Gardens accompanied by dozens of brass bands. At the head of the procession, in the first carriage, was the hero of the hour, Daniel Adamson and to mark the occasion the city's bakers produced a huge loaf with the words 'Daniel Adamson' on it. His personal identification with the project was so strong that for years to come it was known to many as 'Adamson's canal'.

On the day of the procession to Belle Vue it just so happened that the legendary explorer Henry Morton Stanley – of 'Dr Livingstone I presume' fame – was in Manchester to give a lecture. So great was the hubbub that he thought a revolution had started and it was only when he asked a passerby what was going on that his mind was put at rest.

The next item on the agenda was raising the money. One possible source was the good citizens of Manchester, who, after all, had been energised by the success of Adamson's campaign. It is often assumed that the first wave of popular capitalism was started by the Conservative government of the 1980s. In those years, state enterprises like British Telecom, British Gas and the water companies were sold off to the public with the privatisation process being helped along by massive media campaigns, in which the most memorable advert encouraged people to 'tell Sid' about buying shares.

In fact, popular capitalism started a hundred years before Maggie Thatcher. And it started in Manchester, where 39,000 'Sids' flocked to take up shares in the Manchester Ship Canal Company. The new venture now had more private shareholders than any other company in the world, people who were clearly enthused by the potential of the canal and of Manchester.

Successful though the share issue had been yet more capital was needed if the canal was to be built. In stepped Manchester Corporation, which took enormous political and financial risks to get things moving. The municipal authorities lent the new company £5 million, about a third of the total capital of £15.4 million. Raising such a sum was not easy, even for a city with Manchester's wealth. It helped that the municipal boundaries had been significantly expanded, which brought in thousands of new ratepayers. But it was still necessary not only to hike up the rates (by no less than 26 per cent in three years) but also to borrow heavily, putting the city deeply into debt.

With the legal framework in place and the money in the bank the new company got down to work. A first-rate contractor was essential and one was found: Mr Thomas Andrew Walker, aged sixty, a man with vast experience in major civil-engineering projects. Walker had overseen the building of the Metropolitan and District underground railway in London and had then gone on to complete the Severn Tunnel. Although a highly efficient and meticulous manager he was also a good boss, one who cared for his men. As one chief engineer who had employed him said: 'I know of no contractor who has displayed so much care and solicitude for the comfort and welfare of the workpeople by him, as Mr Walker.'

When the land had been acquired the project was divided into eight sections, each with its own engineer in charge. Railway lines were specially built along the route of the canal in order to deliver building materials and to take away the huge amounts of 'spoil' that the contractors were excavating. As with everything else in this great undertaking, the scale of the railway operation was massive, with the 180 steam locomotives pulling 6,000 wagons over 200 hundred miles of temporary track.

While the latest, cutting-edge technology was deployed there was still no substitute for elbow grease and sheer hard graft when it came to digging and disposing of the millions of tons of soil and rocks along the canal route. A very special breed of men would be needed to get the job done. It was on massive projects like these that the worker known to all and sundry as the navvy came into his own. Walker recruited no less than 16,000 of these itinerant workers, who came from all over the north-west as well as Scotland and Ireland. The navvies were a breed apart. Many were known only by their nicknames, which were nothing if not distinctive: Skeedicks, Moonraker, Fatbuck, Rainbow Ratty and Concertina Cockney are examples of their monikers. Their clothes were equally colourful and a typical outfit would include a white felt hat, velveteen coat, scarlet waistcoat, bright-coloured handkerchief worn round the neck, corduroy breeches and high-laced boots.

Tough, hard-working and supremely efficient Walker's navvy army toiled ten hours a day, five-and-a-half days per week for the equivalent of two pence an hour, giving them a weekly income of about £1.25, which they invariably received cash-in-hand in the nearest pub. This wage, for such a physically draining job, was a pittance, even by the standards of the day, and they still had to find their own food and board, which took more than half their income. As one might expect the working day was long, hard and unremitting: during a shift, the navvy was expected to excavate twelve cubic yards of earth, the equivalent of a trench three feet wide, three feet deep and thirty-six-feet long. Try that in your back garden!

Apart from the backbreaking work, the workers' other major problem was accidental injury: on what was the biggest industrial site in Britain accidents were common, with around twelve major incidents every week. Walker, ever the good employer, set up a chain of first-aid stations and also three hospitals, to which the injured were whisked on one of the contractor's trains. He also appointed a surgeon from Liverpool, Robert Jones, to oversee what was claimed to be the first professional emergency service in Europe. The boss was also considerate to those recuperating from injuries: they were given lighter duties, which led to them being called Walker's Fragments by their workmates.

To accommodate his men – who included many thousands of skilled men, as well as the navvies – Walker built what were effectively little towns complete with tea and coffee rooms, mission halls, churches and resident chaplains and one of the biggest of these 'Walker towns' was at the Stanlow peninsula. While the huts in which the men slept were of a high standard for the time, the navvies were certainly not living in the lap of luxury; with up to thirty men bunking down in a room twenty feet by ten, comfort and privacy were both at a premium. Any gaps in the company's services were supplemented by enterprising locals. These 'suttlers and victuallers', as they were known, sold the workers tea, coffee and snacks. They also put up temporary boarding houses and converted old boats into floating lodging houses.

The excavation and construction process was always technically challenging and frequently downright dangerous. There were several freezing winters in which temperatures plunged to levels at which work was all but impossible. Then there was the constant threat of flooding: there were major floods on the Latchford section, at the Little Bolton cutting and at Barton Locks, all of which wiped out months of work. With massive amounts of spoil being hauled on the temporary railways the potential for accidents was high and one collision of trucks near Ellesmere Port claimed the lives of three workers.

If inclement weather and accidents weren't enough to contend with there was also the spectre of industrial unrest: in 1891 a strike over wages saw scab labour being brought onto the site. The strikers were enraged and a riot duly ensued, with machinery being smashed and a violent confrontation between two thousand workers and the police kicking off in the Pomona area.

Despite the many difficulties Walker and his legions of workers encountered there was great optimism that the canal would be successfully completed. The project gripped the popular imagination and not just in Manchester. Many of the Victorian age's celebrities asked to visit the site, among them the Shah of Persia, the Prince of Wales (the future King Edward VII), the great statesman and prime minister, W. E. Gladstone, and Ferdinand de Lesseps, engineer of the Suez Canal.

Then after seven long years – which included the excavation of 54 million cubic yards, around half the size of the Suez Canal – the work was finally completed. What to some critics down Merseyside way was an 'idle dream' had become a reality. Manchester now had docks to rival any port in the land and they were divided into three main units: west of Trafford Road; Trafford Wharf; and the Pomona Docks. But that tells only part of the story because as the directors of the company boasted, with some justification, the entire length of the canal, all thirty-five miles of it, was for practical purposes a dock.

The magnificent achievement did not go unnoticed by the government, which sent a Treasury warrant to the city's lord mayor making Manchester a customs port – as the jargon goes it would now be a 'lawful point of entry for persons and merchandise'. Sadly, the two men who must be given much of the credit would not be around to see it: the doughty contractor, Thomas Walker, died in 1889, much mourned by his men; while Daniel Adamson, the dynamic leader of the campaign, passed away a year later at the age of 71.

So it came to pass that 1 January 1894 was designated as the day on which the Manchester Ship Canal would open for business. Plans had been made for Queen Victoria to perform the official opening ceremony later in the year and the directors did not wish to detract from that royal event. For that reason the ceremonials were to be very limited on New Year's Day and while fifty thousand tickets were made available to shareholders, members of the public were not expected, or encouraged, to attend. That did not put anyone off. Proud Mancunians were desperate to see merchant ships sailing into their city for the first time. They would not have missed it for the world. They had followed every twist and turn of the project in their newspapers, many had willingly subscribed for shares and they had all accepted huge rises in their rates bills. Not for nothing had it become known as the People's Canal and now the people would not be denied.

When the great day arrived the weather was unseasonably fine, more like spring than mid-winter. That was a surprise in itself as the days leading up to the New Year had been characterised by heavy fog. The good weather undoubtedly meant that the crowd – which was always going to be considerable – would be massive. And so it turned out. The *Manchester Guardian* had a reporter at Trafford wharf and in his dispatch he notes that as the first ships hove into view 'the assemblage . . . had grown to extraordinary proportions. Men and women stood ten and a dozen deep and behind them packed together in close squares hundreds more were mounted on the piles of timber with which the ground is strewn.' Some estimates put the turnout at more than half a million.

The excitement grew to fever pitch as the first vessel was spotted: the *Norseman*, a steam yacht, packed with the canal company's directors and their friends, was approaching Manchester, preceded by a small launch. The *Norseman* was followed by the *Snowdrop*, which was carrying civic dignitaries from Manchester and Salford. The cheers from the assembled throng were deafening and as the first ship to ply the canal reached the wharf some people thought a song was needed to match the dignity of the occasion. The problem was that the crowd could not make up its mind about which ditty would be the most appropriate, as the *Guardian*'s man explains.

> The embarrassment of the people when they tried to find some expression for their emotion was almost pathetic. Some tried a stave of 'Auld Lang Syne' but of course that was hopelessly inappropriate. 'God Save the Queen' promised rather better but that died before it had swollen into anything like a chorus and it was not until someone started 'Rule Britannia' that there was anything like unanimity of mind and voice.

Eventually, as the other ships in the convoy followed the *Norseman* into port, the singing of 'Rule Britannia' gave way to lusty roars of approval, which included three cheers for Daniel Adamson.

The *Guardian* reporter was clearly worried about outbreaks of hooliganism, noting that an observer from London would not form a high opinion of a 'North of England' crowd if he happened upon 'the corner of Deansgate and Blackfriars-street on any popular holiday'. His fears were misplaced and the four hundred police on duty – who were assisted by navvies recruited for the day as special constables – had little to do apart from point people in the right direction.

The crowds were equally large and enthusiastic at Barton, where the Barton Road swing bridge and the aqueduct, the principal engineering features of the project, were located. Thousands had packed onto trains at Exchange Station before being whisked to Eccles and Patricroft, the nearest stations to Barton. As that first convoy of ships approached, thousands crowded onto both sides of the canal in anticipation. To add to the sense of occasion a band played a selection of tunes, including 'See the Conquering Heroes Come'. Then about half-past eleven gathering clouds of steam and the sounds of whistles indicated that the little flotilla was fast approaching. The *Guardian* man takes up the story.

> The aqueduct was the first to move, and the people cheered loudly as it was set in motion by hydraulic machinery. The great caisson [a watertight chamber], 252 feet long, six feet deep, and ten feet wide, with its accompanying footway and iron girders and great bulk of water, weighing altogether about 1,500 tons, swung gracefully round on its pivot. The road bridge in the same smooth and noiseless fashion parted asunder and moved into position and the way was clear for the ships which were now seen approaching.

That first opening of the Barton Aqueduct symbolises everything about Manchester and its great ship canal. Financial clout, technological expertise and sheer determination to get the job done had combined in the greatest engineering feat of the Victorian age, an age that did not want for achievements in that sphere.

The opening of the ship canal made Manchester and Salford one of the leading centres for trade, enabling the conurbation to capture around 5 per cent of the total value of British imports and exports by 1914. It also led to an immediate reduction in distribution costs for the city's businesses, a reduction that some historians put at close to £2 million per annum, a huge sum for the time. That was clearly of benefit to the cotton industry, but there were other significant spinoffs.

Manchester became the world's greatest engineering city, particularly in the specialised field of machinery designed for the cotton industry, which it exported to all four corners of the globe. In 1897 the Trafford Park industrial estate was established, the first such estate to be built anywhere, and very close to the ship canal. Manchester also became pre-eminent in the distributive trades and in business finance, developing into what one historian describes as a 'great tentacular city'.

The successful development of the ship canal inspired other cities, at home and abroad, to emulate Manchester. Birmingham, Sheffield and Blackburn, among many others, made firm plans for canal projects. So too did European cities, including Marseille, Rotterdam and Brussels. While in North America, Michigan–Detroit and New York–Philadelphia canals were mooted. The pioneering Manchester Ship Canal Company did not rest on its laurels. It branched out, becoming a railway operator, a major landlord, a property developer and even a bank. Manchester Corporation continued to play an important in the affairs of the company, a link that was strengthened by the passing by Parliament of the Manchester Ship Canal (Finance) Act of 1904.

On 21 May 1894, on a ship called the *Enchantress*, Queen Victoria sailed along the canal, and declared it officially open. Later, on board that vessel, she knighted Councillor Anthony Marshall, the Lord Mayor of Manchester, and Alderman Bailey, Mayor of Salford. The royal seal of approval had been extended to Manchester and how deserved that accolade was. It had taken a concerted effort from everyone in the city to pull off what had seemed an impossible dream and despite the many obstacles put in its way Manchester had not faltered. Never before had a city put aside its differences in such a single-minded way. As one expert, Roderick Grant, notes in his book on the ship canal, it was nothing less than an 'act of faith on behalf of the working people of the city and district who donated money from their earnings to help finance its construction, uniting them with merchants and mill owners, and, eventually, the city's Corporation. Their faith was justified and amply rewarded.'

13

JOLLYWOOD

From a twenty-first century perspective, it might be hard to believe that Manchester once had its own thriving film studio, one that regularly churned out box-office hits. It may not have been on the same scale as Paramount or Warner Brothers, but it made dozens of successful features and for the people of Manchester, it was their very own corner of Hollywood. The city has long been a major hub for television, and both Granada Television and the BBC have had studios in Manchester for several decades. However, neither station laid down roots as early as 1908, when the venture that would become Mancunian Film Corporation began. In fact, both the BBC and Granada owe the now defunct MFC a huge debt, as will become apparent later.

Manchester's film industry was, in essence, the creation of one pioneering family: the Blakeleys. The dynasty was founded by James Blakeley, a market trader and draper who lived on Wainwright Street in Ardwick. Although he had Jewish roots he brought up his two sons, John and James junior, as Roman Catholics, the faith of their mother. Blakeley was what might today be called a serial entrepreneur, someone always looking to branch out, on the trail of the next big thing. One possibility was the film industry, which was beginning to show signs of growth, with the first 'moving picture' being screened in Manchester in 1896. The new medium was an instant hit and customers eager for entertainment flocked to the 'penny gaffs', as early cinemas were known.

James Blakeley was quick to see the opportunity that the movies offered. In 1908 he opened his first penny gaff, in Warrington, in a converted shop, and within a couple of years had three more: in

Levenshulme, Salford and Northwich. He was riding the crest of a very powerful wave: by 1911, Manchester had more cinemas per head of population than anywhere else in the country; no less than 111 for its population of 714,000. A new type of business sprang up to service the picture house: the film renter, what we would today call a distributor. Chief among their number was the always enterprising Blakeley family, whose Central Film Agency was established in 1912, operating from premises on Great Ducie Street. Thanks to the popularity of movies, the business quickly prospered, but profits shot through the roof after John (or John E as he was often called) persuaded his father to take on a silent movie entitled *Tillie's Punctured Romance*, which came out in 1915. It was a film that rival rental companies felt was too long, predicting it would struggle to maintain an audience's interest.

The collective dismissal of *Tillie's* by their rivals gave Central Film Agency exclusive rights in the north-west. CFA must have found the rejection by the other renters mystifying, considering this was Charlie Chaplin's first feature-length comedy. The Blakeleys took a calculated gamble and John E's hunch was right on the money. Chaplin was one of the biggest stars in the world and had appeared in more than thirty shorts since his beloved portrayal as the 'Little Tramp'. *Tillie's Punctured Romance* – produced by the Keystone Film Company and also featuring the legendary Keystone Cops – was a runaway success and was the making of CFA, who pretty much cleaned up in the process.

John E. Blakeley was never one to rest on his laurels and by the early 1930s he had persuaded his family to diversify. Thanks to his track record, it didn't take much to convince them to invest, and this time the plan was to make their own movies. John E. had become frustrated by the charges levied by production companies for their product. He had also grown tired of the dismissive attitude of the London studio bosses to the north of England, its actors and his ambitious plans. The reaction to his studio plans from down south was entirely what he had expected, but it only made him even more determined to wipe the smug smiles off their faces. Producing feature films was a risky and expensive venture, and it would either make or break the company, but they had the finance, and the nerve, to undertake it.

Blakeley's master plan was to make 'Northern films for Northern people in the North'. So it was that in 1934 he set up the Mancunian Film Corporation, almost always referred to as Mancunian Films, which would be run from offices at 54 Deansgate. John E. had a clear vision of his target audience: working-class Northerners who wanted to see their culture and values represented on screen. He found the material for films on his doorstep, in the music halls and theatres of Lancashire. One of his favourite turns was George Formby, who had created the much-loved character John Willie. However, it would be Formby's son, George Formby junior, who would get the opportunity to star in MFC's first feature, *Boots! Boots!* In the film, John Willie is a boot boy at the Crestonia Hotel, in love with scullery maid Snooky. But the plot was secondary to its main purpose, which was to highlight Formby's musical and comedic talents in a series of little sketches and vignettes.

Although Blakeley would later dismiss *Boots! Boots!* as a 'lousy film' it did exceptionally well in the North – if not in the rest of the country – which no doubt led to Formby reprising the role of John Willie in Mancunian's second feature *Off the Dole*. This too was little more than a series of musical and comedy sketches but it included many well-known songs, in particular Formby's 'With My Little Ukulele in My Hand', the ultimate in double entendre. *Off the Dole* was also a hit, although once again its popularity increased the further north one travelled.

Like Formby, many of Blakeley's stars came straight from music-hall, men like Roy Barbour, Barry Barnes and Fred Walmsley, and they were loved by audiences. However, it was another Lancastrian comic who became Mancunian's biggest star and the man who would eventually take its films to a wider audience, outside of its Northern redoubts. His name was Frank Randle. Born in the village of New Springs near Wigan in 1901, Randle had become the most popular comedian north of Birmingham. His catchphrases, always couched in his thick Lancastrian accent, were legendary:

> 'Gerroff mi foot'
> 'I've supped some ale toneet'
> 'She's a hottun'

He had many stage personas, perhaps the best-known being Old Hiker. For this eccentric character, Randle dressed up as an overgrown boy scout in khaki shorts and, beer bottle in hand, Old Hiker would regale audiences with his escapades, belching furiously all the while. His critics found him crude and his characters were invariably lecherous, drunken or violent, or indeed a combination of all three, and there were many battles with authority concerning the risqué elements of his act. These included a long-running feud with the police chief of Blackpool in the course of which, it is said, the bold Frank hired a plane and bombed the seaside town with toilet rolls.

The thread that ran through Randle both in his act and in his private life was a determination to live life as he saw fit, and not be bound by convention. Decades before rock stars smashed up hotels rooms Frank Randle was paving the way, taking an axe to his dressing room after brushes with theatre managers or censors. On one occasion he fired a loaded revolver at an extra on a film set. And woe-betide anyone who dared to heckle him during his act, which he would respond to by taking out his false teeth and hurling them at the miscreant.

For his part, he never accepted that he went over the top, explaining that 'I'm vulgar but not filthy,' a fine distinction that many found hard to grasp. Of course audiences loved him, especially in Lancashire and Yorkshire, and they packed out his shows. Blakeley realised that he was a natural for the big screen and for Mancunian Films. His best known feature for the company was 1940's *Somewhere in England*, a huge hit, and it was followed by several sequels, including *Somewhere in Camp* and *Somewhere on Leave*. This was wartime and in the *Somewhere* movies he would play enlisted men who saw as it as their sole purpose in life to undermine the officer class. The following extract gives a flavour of the humour:

> Officer: 'Now my man. What were you in civilian life?'
> Randle: 'Who me?'
> Officer: 'Yes you.'
> Randle: 'Oh you mean when I was working for a living.'
> Officer: 'Yes when you were working.'
> Randle: 'Oh, I used to train performing fleas.'
> Officer: 'Performing fleas. You had to scratch for a living, eh.'

Despite the success of Mancunian's films it would not be until 1947 that it was able to make films in its home city. The capital needed for such a project was enormous and it was only with the help of outside investors that Blakeley was able to put together the necessary finance. His backers included Jimmy Brennan, a scrap-metal dealer and cinema owner, and also Frank Randle, who became a director of the new enterprise, which was registered as Film Studios Manchester Ltd. Blakeley looked around the city for premises and paid £70,000 for an old Wesleyan church on Dickenson Road, Rusholme, spending another £15,000 on refurbishments. A total sum of £85,000 might not sound that much but it was the equivalent of several million in today's money. So it was that almost forty years after his father, James Blakeley, had set up his first penny gaff, the circle was now complete. Manchester was ready to make its first feature film.

George Formby officially opened the studio doors for business in front of an excited crowd of locals, celebrities and press. In the years that followed a string of cheap and cheerful movies, mostly comedies, were churned out. The nature of the output from Dickenson Road led locals to call it 'The Fun Factory', while in later years it was nicknamed 'Jollywood', for the same reason.

The city was on the map as far as the film industry was concerned and given Manchester's obsession with football, it was perhaps fitting that the first feature film to be released was *Cup-Tie Honeymoon*. Made on a budget of £45,000, it was a burlesque musical; an unusual mixture of football and romance starring Sandy Powell, Dan Young, Betty Jumel and a very young Pat Pilkington – later to become Pat Phoenix, who would go on to have enormous success as *Coronation Street*'s Elsie Tanner – as Powell's wife. With several scenes filmed at Manchester City's Maine Road stadium, the film was released to coincide with the 1948/49 football season and garnered plenty of local interest. Of course, the critics, largely southern-based, hated it, as they did virtually every other film made in Rusholme. But audiences couldn't have cared less what the southern papers said; they lapped it up.

It was part of a distinct trend. Mancunian's movies – usually churned out in less than five weeks on shoestring budgets – often dwarfed Hollywood blockbusters starring the likes of Marlene Dietrich and Errol Flynn at the box office, particularly in the North. Many future household names would make their debut on the silver screen thanks to the Dickenson Road studios. They included the likes of Josef Locke,

Norman Evans, Jimmy James, Jimmy Clitheroe, Bernard Youens, Diana Dors and Tessie O'Shea.

Extras would literally be dragged in off the street and, for a small fee, local residents would even lend furniture for the sets. It was truly a Mancunian product in every sense of that word. During a preview screening of one film, the following conversation was overheard:

> 'That looks just like your front room, Mary.'
> 'That *is* my front room,' came the reply.

Local actor Arthur McNuff was enlisted to be an extra in several of the studio's movies, although his most important role had nothing to do with acting. It was McNuff's job to go out and find Irish-tenor-turned-actor Josef Locke, a regular in Blakeley's movies. The man from the Emerald Isle could invariably be found propping up a bar in any one of the local watering holes, although the Welcome pub on the corner of Dickenson Road and Wilmslow Road was a particular favourite of both Locke and other members of the cast and crew.

Locke, despite his fondness for ale, became a big star. His first film for Mancunian was *Holidays with Pay*, released in 1948, and which also starred Frank Randle. It tells the story of the Rogers family who set off for a holiday in Blackpool where they have many adventures, including one in a haunted house. Apart for the comedy it was notable for Locke's rendition of popular songs, among them 'I'll Take You Home Again, Kathleen'. *Holidays with Pay* was a huge hit right across the country, prompting many critics to lambast the British film industry, and especially J. Arthur Rank, for its elitism and lack of empathy with popular taste. The headline in the *Sunday People* said it all: 'Mr Rank, they want Randle not Shakespeare,' was the blunt message.

Blakeley became almost a one-man film studio, writing, directing and producing most of Mancunian's films. Known as 'Pop' or 'Dad' to the staff he was ever present in Dickenson Road, instantly recognisable thanks to the Homburg hat that seemed to be irremovably attached to his head. There would be times when there was no script as such and John E. would simply instruct the actors to 'be funny' in front of the camera. Of course, he was on pretty solid ground when telling that to the likes of George Formby and Frank Randle, both comic geniuses. In fact, Blakeley was one of the few men who could handle the big names confidently and while there were often heated arguments with Randle he never let his star attraction get the better of him. That took some doing with a character as volatile as Frank Randle, who, as the years passed, grew greatly to respect his head of studio.

Randle continued to be the studio's main attraction, going on to star in several more features including *School For Randle* and *It's A Grand Life* (which featured 22-year-old blonde bombshell Diana Dors), all of which made more than decent returns. Being on the studio's board of directors, Randle had a vested interest in the films being successful, aside from boosting his own popularity. He had creative licence to influence the films to his liking and each picture was a perfect vehicle to suit his own ribald style.

Mancunian was becoming a major player in the British film industry. It could reasonably be argued that one of Britain's most enduring film franchises had its origins in the city, with the 1949 release of *What a Carry On* – unofficially the first in the series and starring Josef Locke and Jimmy Jewel – being made on Dickenson Road. The fledgling Hammer Film Productions – soon to become the cult, quintessentially British, Hammer Horror Company – also used the studios to make several pictures before eventually moving their operation south. Several locations around Manchester were used extensively by Mancunian, including the Refuge Building, site of an explosive end to the 1960 Stanley Baker epic, *Hell Is a City*. The sprawling Xaverian College campus just a stone's throw from Dickenson Road was also a regular backdrop.

Sadly, the global hit that the studio desperately craved eluded it and in 1953, following the release of *It's A Grand Life*, the cameras stopped rolling as filming at Dickenson Road finally came to a close. John E. Blakeley was now 65 and had come to the conclusion that he'd done his bit for Manchester. He retired to enjoy the company of his grandchildren before it was too late. He had directed fifteen movies, written thirteen and produced a total of thirty-two in just twenty-six years; proof, if proof be needed, that this most prolific of film moguls deserved a break. He also realised, visionary that he was, that the new and burgeoning medium of television would provide the film industry with very stiff competition.

Interestingly, and despite the continual panning by London-based critics, of all the films Blakeley produced, not one lost money. How many producers would kill to have that on their CV? It is a fantastic epitaph for Mancunian and provides further evidence of what a genius John E. Blakeley really was. In 1954 he sold his cherished company, the business he'd put his heart and soul into for the best part of forty-five years, to the BBC, thus making Dickenson Road the corporation's first regional studio and soon to be home to the likes of *Top of the Pops* and *Grandstand*. The Beeb, which drew heavily on Mancunian's technical expertise, would remain on the premises until 1975.

One of Mancunian's greatest assets, Frank Randle, died in 1957 from gastroenteritis and alcohol abuse and a year later, John E. Blakeley, a largely unheralded visionary of British cinema, died too. Many of Mancunian's technicians, cameramen and other members of the production staff soon found employment with the new owners and several began working for what became the embryonic Granada Television in the city centre. In many ways, the Blakeley family's legacy lived on and but for them putting Manchester on the cinematic map, perhaps the BBC and Granada would have gone elsewhere.

However, Mancunian Films wasn't quite ready to hang up the clapboard and thanks to Blakeley's son, Tom, it continued to produce films in London until the mid-Sixties. In fact, John E. was credited as associate producer for the 1960 film *Trouble with Eve* – two years after his death. Tom carried on the family tradition by releasing a succession of profitable B-movie crime pictures before eventually ceasing operations completely. Having produced a total of over sixty movies, half of which were features, it is a pity that the nation seems to have forgotten this bold project and the enterprising individuals behind it. They proved there was life for British cinema outside the capital. The people of Manchester should feel proud of the Blakeley family's achievements.

The studio's archives were seriously depleted when a fire tore through Kay Laboratories in 1980. The blaze destroyed all of the nitrate master copies of the films made in the 1940s and 1950s. It was only by chance that John E. Blakeley's grandson, Mike, discovered most of the 35-mm originals while clearing out a vault in the Parsonage, Manchester, which was the original headquarters of Mancunian. Mike Blakeley is now working on a project that will bring together copies of all the films made by Mancunian, as well as those made by his grandfather prior to setting the studios up. This unique collection will be based, and rightly so, in Manchester. Mike, a former Granada cameraman, scoured the globe for copies of the lost gems and has sourced many of the films from private collectors, the British Film Institute and Paramount Studios. He is hopeful that, with the invaluable help of the Northwest Film Archive and the Manchester Metropolitan University, the Blakeley family's heritage will be available for the people of the city to enjoy.

Today, all that remains of the Dickenson Road studio is a plaque on the wall of a house built on the site of the old church. The current owners claim that, on a quiet day, you can occasionally still hear the echoes of 'action!' the sound of a clapboard snapping and even the smell of greasepaint . . .

14

WILL THE REAL BERNARD MANNING PLEASE STAND UP?

'Two nuns riding down a cobbled street, one turns to the other and says, "I've never come this way before" . . .'

'There were two Jews, Eli and Hymie, walking along a street in Glasgow. They saw a gang of skinheads coming towards them. Eli turns to Hymie and says, "Here's that £500 I owe you."'

'I had a relative who died at Auschwitz. He fell out of the watchtower.'

Whether those are Bernard Manning jokes or not, they are certainly in his territory and one of Britain's most famous comedians would have brought the house down with them. The trouble with Manning was that, towards the end of his life, you didn't know whether to laugh or cry. On the one hand he was pilloried in the press, subjected to undercover filming and dismissed as an overweight bigot, while on the other he was feted as a comic genius and tireless charity fundraiser.

Will the real Bernard Manning please stand up?

In effect, he had two careers. There were the early years, when he toured working men's clubs, appeared at his club in Harpurhey and became a star of 1970s television. Then there were the later years, when alternative comedy arrived with a host of young, politically correct comedians, helping to kill off his television career. That said, he was often his own worst enemy when it came to performing in front of the cameras. His style of comedy, adored by the white working-class audiences of the North in the Sixties, became an albatross around his neck, but one he wore out of choice. Doors slammed shut as some audiences turned their back on the racist, anti-Semitic and sexist jokes his act was based on. To some he had become a dinosaur, a comedian from another age.

He was an easy target, but he put himself up there to be shot at by refusing to change. 'I am what I am,' he would tell his family and friends when he was vilified by the media, 'I can't change now.' Yet many insist he was a warm, gentle man, a devoted father, husband and son and somebody who raised millions for charity without publicity.

Whose perception is correct?

Born of Russian Jewish ancestry in Ancoats on 13 August 1930, Manning was raised as a strict Catholic. He attended Mount Carmel Roman Catholic elementary school in Blackley for the first time in 1935 and his chubby frame soon earned him the nickname 'Fat Manning'. The next trauma he suffered was slightly more serious: the Second World War. Manning recalls the blitz that the Nazis inflicted on the city.

> In 1941, I was ten and I can remember cowering under the stairs with my mum when the bombs were raining down. There was hardly a building left standing in Manchester and everything was in darkness except for the fires from the buildings. When you opened the door, the sky was red with burning shrapnel and the sound of the bombers sent shivers through you. When I look back, I wonder how we all got through it.

He was an unremarkable student and left school at the age of fourteen to work at Gallaher's tobacco factory in Derby Road, Cheetham Hill, which made Senior Service cigarettes. The factory was staffed mainly by women, this being 1944 and most men away at war. Bernard was a grinder's mate, sharpening the knives that were used to cut tobacco. Life on the shop floor was far from a picnic; it was a highly regimented environment in which the workers were expected to graft hard for their modest wages. The young Manning literally had his nose to the grindstone but he found an escape from the restrictions of factory life as a singer in pub-talent competitions, many of which he won thanks to his excellent voice. That in turn led to bookings at pubs and clubs and even as a semi-pro he earned more from his showbiz outings than he did at Gallaher's. Thanks to his new found-status he was able to wave goodbye to the grinding machine and support himself through singing, supplementing his income when necessary by helping out in his dad's greengrocer business.

After the war, the requirement to do national service took him into the army and he served as a soldier in the Manchester Regiment. Based for a time at Spandau prison in Berlin – where senior Nazis like Rudolf Hess and Admiral Doenitz were incarcerated – Manning would sing the popular songs of the day to entertain his peers and their positive response led to him putting on weekend shows. Initially free of charge, he began to sell tickets and the seed of an idea was firmly planted.

His singing career blossomed. So much so that when he completed his tour of duty he turned professional, becoming a popular compère during the early 1950s. He also fronted a number of big bands of the day, including the Oscar Rabin band. He had a fine singing voice and could carry a ballad with a surprisingly extensive vocal range, but it was as a compère that he shone. Thanks to a razor-sharp wit and impecc-able comic timing he took his first steps into stand-up.

> I used to work at the Northern Sporting Club just down the road from where I would buy the house and live at in Alkrington. I started putting a few gags in my act, but they weren't just gags, they were jokes with a little bit of stab in them as well. Nobody had ever done that before in Britain. There were all these little soft comics who were frightened of saying boo on stage. And I came along with humour that took your feet from right under you.

That was an understatement. In his own way, he was the alternative comedian of the day; one of a new breed who pioneered adult humour and explicit material. He cut his teeth in the unforgiving environment of working men's clubs around the north of England and honed his act accordingly. He was always crystal clear about who his audience were and what they wanted, as he later explained to a journalist: '*Jackanory* stuff is for wimps. Grown men that worked on building sites don't want to hear "Ecky Thumps" and "ooh dammits".' He was hated by the politically correct classes, typified by *Guardian* readers, and so, quite naturally, the punters loved him.

Things were also looking up in his personal life. In 1949 he met

Veronica Finnerann, 'Vera', a pretty blonde secretary who worked in a cotton mill. She was a fan of his singing and one night she complimented him on his rendition of 'Autumn Leaves', which just happened to be her favourite song. They went steady from that night on, although it took another seven years, until 1956, for them to tie the knot. Manning would later joke that he always remembered the year he got married . . . because it was the year Manchester City won the FA Cup. Of course he really was only joking because they were well matched and Vera was the love of his life for more than forty years.

Now that he had found a winning formula both on and off the stage, he borrowed £30,000 from his father to buy and refurbish the Embassy Club on Rochdale Road in Harpurhey, turning it from a from a billiard hall to a working man's club. The Embassy opened in 1959 and proved the saying 'If you build it, they will come.' The venue quickly became a Mecca for the people that surrounded its painted white walls and within a short space of time his income leapt from hundreds of pounds a week to thousands. In years to come, it would be the only place to go for large groups of men on nights out, ranging from works dos to stag parties, as well as those keen to see what all the fuss was about.

Matt Monro, Mike Yarwood, Jimmy Tarbuck, Vince Hill and – so Manning claimed – the Beatles, all played the Embassy Club, which became a prestigious venue during its 1960s heyday. Dressed as the 'darts player from hell' Manning found that racist and sexist jokes went down a treat, though in fairness, most comics who toured the working men's circuits used similar material. His career was given a boost of rocket-fuel proportions by the massive changes in British society. A huge influx of Asian and West Indian people was initially welcomed, but later resented, and this provided an endless stream of material for Manning, who had an uncanny ability to tap into the psyche of the man in the street. By targeting black men and Pakistanis, he was giving the public what it wanted, reassuring them that the immigrants were second-class citizens, there to be poked fun at. His argument was that if they wanted to try their luck in this country and take the jobs of the indigenous population they were fair game.

His defence would always be that what he said on stage was just comedy and that it wasn't only minorities that were being targeted;

everyone was fair game, except kids, the handicapped, and, for some strange reason, mothers-in-law. Then, Manning's career kicked into over-drive. In June 1971, Granada Television launched *The Comedians*, which was a half-hour showcase for stand-ups, most of whom had a following in the North, but were little known in the rest of Britain. In its two-year life the show was a major success, second only to *Coronation Street* in the ratings and Bernard Manning – along with fellow performers Charlie Williams, Duggie Brown, Russ Abbot, Stan Boardman, Jim Bowen, Frank Carson, Mick Miller and Mike Reid – shot to national prominence.

His style on *The Comedians* was unusual, as his biographer Jonathan Margolis relates: 'He stood out for his deadpan manner and the way he didn't laugh at his own jokes, as a lot of the other comedians did. He did not interact with the audience directly, but just fired gag after gag, punctuated by a lazy drag on his cigar.' (*Bernard Manning: A Biography*, published in 1996)

Ironically, the Race Relations Board applauded the format because it gave black comedian Charlie Williams the opportunity to get his own back on right-wing politicians such as Enoch Powell. It never really got out of hand because the limitations television placed on the acts meant that the material wasn't all that controversial, although to keep audiences happy there were plenty of 'Englishman, Irishman and Scotsman' jokes.

The show had many spinoffs, such as a hit album, sell-out theatrical versions and lucrative personal appearances. It made the careers of dozens of acts who might otherwise been confined to the clubs and pubs they had previously scratched a living in. The highlight was a season at the Palladium in London, which agreed to host *The Comedians* for six weeks, a run that was later extended to five-and-a-half months. Manning must have thought he had died and gone to heaven: he had dreamt of appearing at the great London theatre ever since he got into the business. There was an even bigger thrill to come: during the Palladium run the cast of *The Comedians* was invited to perform at a Royal Command Performance and after the show Bernard got to shake hands with the Queen. 'I love meeting famous people so being intro-duced to the Queen was the greatest thrill of my life,' he later exulted.

But this still wasn't enough for Granada's head of light entertainment John Hamp, who had devised *The Comedians*, or for Bernard Manning. Hamp didn't see Harpurhey's finest merely as a parochial talent and he arranged for his protégé to perform at the prestigious MGM Grand in Las Vegas, in which Bernard would appear on the same bill as Dean Martin. It was designed as a one-night-only event, but it was something Manning was incredibly proud of and he would often refer to the show later in his career, particularly when he was under attack.

Manning's arrival Stateside coincided with the impeachment of President Richard Nixon and he adapted his act surprisingly well for a US audience, which had never seen the like. He criticised the politicians for merely removing Nixon from office and suggested instead that Teddy Kennedy should have been asked to drive him home. Spotting several Japanese tourists in the crowd, he remarked: 'Don't forget Pearl Harbor. December 1941, you fucking bastards,' and then said to another audience member, 'You look like a nice fella, come and piss on this Jap over here.' Bernard Manning was being Bernard Manning and he swapped Irish jokes for Polack gags, proving that his comedy was universal.

American agents queued to sign him up for a season at a casino on the famous Las Vegas Strip, but there was a problem. Manning never liked to be away from home for too long, hated sleeping in a strange bed and didn't enjoy the stifling Nevada heat. Whether he would have cracked Vegas, we will never know; he would certainly have made an impact of some sorts, even it was for being served with a deportation order! He also turned down £10,000 for a one-off show in Dubai, claiming it was 'too hot'.

One thing was for certain, you could take the boy out of Manchester, but you could never take Manchester out of the boy.

Back home, thanks to the publicity generated by *The Comedians*, the crowds flocked in even greater numbers to the Embassy Club to see him perform live and few left disappointed. A workaholic, he took on gigs up and down the country, in addition to his stints at the Embassy. With the money pouring in life was good. In 1974, Manning became a regular compère on Granada Television's *The Wheeltappers and Shunters*

Social Club, which ran for three years and further exposed Manning to a national audience.

Along with success came the trappings of fame: a luxurious house (just a stone's throw from his club), a Rolls Royce and plenty of money to lavish on wife Vera and son Bernard Junior. Indeed, it was said that he managed to accumulate a fortune of £5 million.

It seemed he could do no wrong.

But times were changing as the tide of immigrants from the Commonwealth grew stronger and the new arrivals asserted themselves politically and socially. This was reflected in the cultural sphere, as complaints about racially provocative shows such as *Till Death Us Do Part* and *Love Thy Neighbour* became legion and eventually both shows were axed. While many of his fellow Northern comics took note and fine tuned their acts, Manning carried on regardless, refusing to bend the knee. In fact there was nothing he loved more than tormenting his critics. When a female journalist from *The Guardian* pitched up at the Embassy Club – no doubt with the intention of writing a hatchet piece – Manning put her right next to the stage. During his act he was as provocative as ever, telling the woman that she 'looked like something out of the *Addams Family*' and 'that she needed a good shag'.

Manning always argued his material was designed to make people laugh and that there was no malice in it, denying throughout his life that he was a racist. But his unwillingness to move with the times was starting to affect his work and his small-screen appearances became infrequent as a new breed of comics appeared during the mid-1980s, many encouraged by new television station Channel 4.

Ben Elton, French and Saunders, Rik Mayall and a host of other new stand-ups poked fun at the establishment, but had grown up in a different era, one in which it was no longer acceptable to poke fun at someone because of their religion or skin colour. The new breed despised the old guard and although Manning was a particular target, he steadfastly refused to change. The audiences that continued to pack the Embassy Club suggested there was still a thirst for his gags.

But while the laughs were plentiful, in 1986 he suffered a great loss: his devoted wife Vera died and some say he was never the same again. In an interview a decade later he recalled what happened.

She was on a cruise in Naples. She had a heart attack and I got to hear about it ten minutes before I was due to go on stage. Can you imagine that? Jesus, that was one of the worst nights of my life. I went on, did my act and then collapsed as soon as I came off stage.

Three weeks later, Vera died.

'Nobody knows,' he said. 'You can't explain the grief to anybody. It's with you first thing in the morning and last thing at night. The only time I can really forget about it is when I'm on stage.'

He continued to tour, but his television appearances were becoming fewer by the year and when he did make it on to the box, it made for awkward viewing. Invited to appear on Terry Wogan's chat show on BBC Television he refused to tone down his act. In fact, during that edition of *Wogan* he told so many racist jokes and uttered so many expletives that the BBC switchboard went into meltdown. Mary Whitehouse, that guardian of morality, demanded an apology, which of course he refused to give. Criticism only served to embolden Barnard Manning.

There was worse to come.

In 1995 the award-winning documentary team at Granada Television's *World in Action* secretly filmed Manning at a gentleman's fundraiser at Haydock Park, which was attended by a number of Greater Manchester police officers. While Manning targeted the only black police officer in attendance, the cameras rolled and the die was cast. When the show aired, Greater Manchester Police chief constable David Wilmot condemned the comedian's tirade and also the wisdom of his officers for attending a show that was always going to be in the worst possible taste. Manning was once again making headlines for all the wrong reasons and was even condemned by John Major, the then prime minister.

During the show, Manning had asked the black officer: 'Isn't it better than swinging in trees?' Then, in an aside to the audience, he remarked, 'They actually think because they are born here they are English. That means if a dog is born in a stable, it's a horse.'

Offensive? Yes. Racist? Absolutely. Typical Manning? Most certainly.

The officer in question, 34-year-old David McIntosh, would later say, 'I didn't feel a victim. Everyone came under attack: Scousers, Jews . . .'

In his defence, Manning argued: 'I'm not a racist. I recently did a show to send a terminally ill Pakistani boy to Disneyland.' But his critics weren't interested. They smelled fresh blood and moved in for the kill.

By contrast his legions of fans stayed faithful and so the Embassy Club sailed towards its fortieth anniversary still playing to packed houses every Thursday, Friday and Saturday night when Bernard was on stage. Elsewhere, the reaction was not entirely supportive and a gig at Willesden Comedy Palace in London was axed shortly after the *World in Action* programme. It followed dozens of complaints from the local Asian community. There were threats, too, and Oxford Apollo was warned it would be firebombed if Manning appeared, while around the same time another gig was cancelled in Hastings after yet more complaints.

There was another unfortunate incident in 1995 when he was performing at a club in Derby. During his act he harangued two black waitresses about the size of black men's penises, which left them understandably upset. They took their complaints to the Commission for Racial Equality, which funded an unfair-dismissal case against their employers, a case the two women won.

These were testing times for Manning, who would lose two of his brothers and beloved 95-year-old mother, Mary Ellen, within the space of a few weeks in 1995. But for his son, he may have given up altogether. Instead, he found solace on stage, where he could forget his heartaches amidst the laughter of the crowd.

Former Manchester City legend Mike Summerbee leapt to Manning's defence at the height of the furore.

> The people of Manchester know Bernard for what he is. They love him for his entertainment and charity work. If there's ever anyone in need, Bernard's always the first to offer to help out. If you took a vote among the people of Manchester about all the recent controversy, the result would be overwhelmingly in Bernard's favour.

But there were choppy seas ahead and while the people of Manchester defended him, he was targeted by other showbiz figures. The most notable was Caroline Aherne during a highly controversial episode of *The Mrs Merton Show*. It was old school versus alternative comedy and Manning came out of it wounded and with his career irreparably damaged. Aherne, in her acerbic alter-ego as the ageing host, rode the

Manning jibes, bided her time and was more than a match for her quarry, who had the audience in stitches with a series of jokes. But a distinct sense of unease pervaded throughout, especially when *One Foot in the Grave* star Richard Wilson, a fellow guest, was the butt of numerous Manning put downs and was clearly far from amused.

In the certain knowledge that Aherne would fight fire with fire, Manning came out with all guns blazing but his constant references to how much charity work he undertook seemed to be his way of saying, 'Yes, I know I offend a lot of people, but I raise money for the needy so it's okay.' Maybe he had a point. Maybe not.

Eventually, Aherne cut to the chase: 'The thing about you Bernard is you're a racist, aren't you?'

Manning had spent much of his life rejecting this accusation, so it was a shock when he replied, 'Yes. There are some people I like and some I don't.' He made matters even worse for himself when he declared: 'There were no Pakis at Dunkirk.'

He later retracted his words, claiming he had been joking and that the whole interview had been nothing more than a wind-up, but in many people's eyes, Bernard Manning had allowed the mask to slip. If he really had been playing a game, it had backfired spectacularly. Perhaps Richard Wilson's dismissive comment earlier in the show of 'Bernard who?' had got to him. He had lowered his guard, inwardly seething with rage in a studio in which he had come to the fore in *The Comedians*, almost three decades earlier. The studio that had spawned his on-screen career had sealed his fate.

Hundreds of viewers called to complain, particularly about Manning's claim that black and Asian men had not fought for Britain in the Second World War, but the BBC defended the programme, arguing that it was important to show both facets of his personality. Bernard Manning would spend the rest of his career defending his routine and being vilified for his stubborn refusal to change his ways. His defence rested mainly on his charity work and the fact that an important part of it was raising money for high-profile black sportsmen such as cricketers Faroukh Engineer and Clive Lloyd and Manchester City goalkeeper Alex Williams.

In his biography of Manning, Jonathan Margolis – who spent around eighteen months interviewing the comic, his family and his associates – cites many instances of his subject's generosity. For example, at one sportsmen's dinner in Manchester the aim was to raise £4,000 from an auction so that the Variety Club of Great Britain could buy a coach to take disabled children on holiday. When only £500 was raised, Manning, who was the auctioneer, announced that he would put in the £3,500 that was still needed.

On another occasion a close pal, Larry Jason (known as Josser), was taken seriously ill. Josser owed money to many people but he wanted to die knowing that he had cleared his debts. When he heard about his friend's plight, Bernard put on a show at the Embassy Club, printed the tickets and handed over a pile of cash to Josser, along with £500 from his own pocket. Later Josser wrote his benefactor a very touching letter, thanking him for his help at his hour of need, a letter that caused Manning to break down in tears. Margolis also confirms that the story about Bernard Manning sending the terminally ill Asian boy to Disneyland is no work of fiction: it really happened and for his many friends and admirers that is the mark of the man.

However, to his critics, the string of good works mattered not one jot. He had been set up for a fall on *Mrs Merton* and he had taken the bait. For a man renowned for his sharpness on stage, it was a spectacular own goal. For the anti-Manning brigade, it was manna from heaven; nobody in telly land would ever touch him again. Anybody watching his shows from that point on would be condoning the jokes of a racist; anyone who booked him in a theatre would be welcoming a racist. Overnight he became persona non grata in luvviedom.

When he applied for an entertainment licence in 1996, a Rusholme trader objected and had his complaint considered by Manchester city councillors. During the hearing, the complainant, 33-year-old Hitesh Batt, insisted: 'At one time, the material may have been acceptable, but not in 1996. The world has changed.'

Indeed it had and Manning's promise to tone down his act in future was the first public acknowledgment that his jokes were past their sell-by date. In the safe confines of the Embassy Club, however, nothing changed. Within a few weeks he was again in the headlines as an Asian community relations councillor was taken by the *Manchester Evening*

News to judge whether his act had indeed been 'toned down'. It hadn't, despite Manning's claims to the contrary.

By 1998, his health was suffering and he was admitted to hospital for tests after complaining of feeling unwell during a show in Blackpool. Diabetic, overweight and now sixty-seven, the future looked bleak for Britain's most controversial comedian, but he was far from finished. He continued to appear at the Embassy Club until 25 July 1999, when he finally exited stage left for the last time. His failing health meant he could no longer commit to entertaining the masses in the club he'd owned for forty years and his last hour on stage was every bit as controversial as his first. Leave them laughing, as the old saying goes.

The Embassy Club closed its doors for the last time and a chapter of Manchester's history closed, too, though his son would later reopen the venue as a function suite. In his later years, Manning senior found solace and an entirely new audience in the form of DVDs, which netted him a small fortune and proved there was still an appetite for his brand of humour.

He couldn't give the business up completely and enjoyed something of a revival towards the end of his life, appearing in a Channel 4 special for a show in Bombay, playing clubs when he felt well enough and appearing at Marco Pierre White's fortieth birthday party, at which Madonna and Guy Ritchie were among the guests. Peter Kay spent a couple of days in Manning's company as he honed the role of Brian Potter in the runaway success that became *Phoenix Nights*. It also transpired that Bernard had an unexpected admirer in Stephen Fry, a pillar of the showbiz liberal elite. Fry, it seemed, admired the technique and comic timing, which prompted the following riposte from the man in question: 'He's a poof of course, but he's got good taste.'

Despite appearances to the contrary, Manning had tired of the constant criticism. His health was failing and his public appearances became ever less frequent. Finally, at 3.10 p.m. on 18 June 2007, the curtain came down on Bernard Manning for the last time when he passed away at the age of seventy-six following a two-week spell in hospital with a kidney disorder. With his devoted son at his bedside, he slipped peacefully away. Right to the end he never lost his sense of humour: when Bernard junior asked him if he wanted to be cremated or buried his irrepressible father replied: 'Surprise me.'

His fans mourned his passing, while others openly celebrated.

One barb came from a most unexpected source. The respected newsreader Sir Trevor McDonald, on the satirical *News Knight* television show, while introducing a slot called 'racist and dead', said: 'This week it's the turn of incompetent, narrow-minded northerner Bernard Manning. Personally, I never thought of Bernard Manning as a racist comic; just a fat, white bastard.'

ITV received two hundred complaints about McDonald's quip, but the one question that couldn't be answered was: what would Bernard have made of it? Ofcom cleared McDonald and ITV of charges of racism, ruling that the joke was justified in context and that he was only parodying Manning. Few could deny it was Manning territory and it might just have made Bernard smile. It was, after all, just a joke, wasn't it?

The people of Manchester kept faith with a favourite son. On 25 June 2007 Bernard Manning made his last appearance on this earth. A hearse pulled away from his home, stopping briefly outside the Embassy Club, where hundreds of local people were waiting. As the funeral party drew up they broke into spontaneous applause. Respects paid, the hearse, which was being pulled by four black horses sporting black-feathered plumes, left for Blackley crematorium where the mourners included fellow comedians Tommy Cannon and Bobby Ball, Jim Bowen, Stan Boardman, Roy Walker and Roy 'Chubby' Brown. The chapel was full, with three hundred mourners packed onto its benches, while a further one hundred and fifty filed into an overflow chapel. Choking back tears the legendary Irish comedian, Frank Carson, who appeared with Manning on *The Comedians*, delivered the eulogy, telling those who had gathered that he had loved the man.

There are a couple of interesting postscripts. It turned out that Manning had written his own obituary, which was published by the *Daily Mail* on 20 June 2007. It is clear that he deeply resented those who for so long had maligned him as a racist and a bigot. It was because of them, he insists, that he was 'kept off mainstream television for years, while filling the airwaves with a bunch of fifth-rate so-called comics who were about as funny as a dose of bird flu and whose acts had all the humour of a funeral parlour. (Trust me, I'm in one now and there's not a laugh to be had anywhere.)' Fulminating against the politically correct elite he goes on to say that the whole point of comedy is 'to make people laugh and that was what I was good at'. He also took the opportunity vehemently to deny he was ever a racist, noting that he had Jewish ancestry himself and had done benefit nights for people from all racial backgrounds.

The other intriguing story that emerged after his death was the acknowledgement that for eighteen years he had been in a secret relationship with Lynn Morgan, a woman thirty years his junior. The couple met in the Embassy Club, two years after the death of his beloved Vera, where Lynn was a cloakroom attendant. It suited both parties to keep it quiet: Lynn because she didn't want her young son to be teased for going out with the famous comedian and Manning because he would have got stick for going out with someone who was so much younger than himself. Morgan confirmed that Manning was a loving, caring, generous human being who told her 'a hundred times a day that he loved me'.

A man who raised millions for charities of all races, creeds and colour; a devoted son, husband, father and grandfather who would unashamedly cry at the drop of a hat when remembering those he had lost or loved. Bernard Manning was an enigma. His gags were from a world the majority of people had gladly left behind, but he just couldn't let go, not while people were still laughing. The world changed but Bernard never did.

Comic genius? Racist? Bigot? Sentimental softy with a heart of gold? Will the real Bernard Manning please stand up?

15

SHOWGROUND OF THE WORLD

There was a time, not that long ago, when Manchester had its very own theme park. In fact, that doesn't go anywhere near doing Belle Vue justice. For the people of northern England, it was the equivalent of Disneyland, a magical escape from everyday life for the millions who flocked though its gates. When it comes to grand projects, Belle Vue sits proudly among Manchester's greatest achievements and the only sad part about this chapter in the city's life is that it no longer exists. In fact, there is no real sign it ever existed at all with the vast area it once occupied now home to new houses and, among other things, a car-auction lot. Yet this was a place of so many firsts, so much invention and imagination. It deserves a more fitting epitaph than a few pleasant memories, the crumbling remains of the odd outbuilding and a ghost railway station. Nobody would ever know that circus acts once performed there, lions roared and steam ships sailed around a huge lake. All forgotten. A distant memory.

The story of the only theme park Manchester ever had is as captivating as the park itself. Belle Vue Zoological Gardens was the brainchild of one man, John Jennison, and his idea for something that was to prove so revolutionary sprang from humble beginnings. In 1829 his eureka moment happened literally in his own backyard. A keen horticulturist and ornithologist, Jennison became fascinated with a family of birds nesting in his garden. After a while, he placed a net over a bush in which a thrush had made its home and laid eggs. The parent, separated from its offspring, continued to feed her chicks through the net and the unusual sight became a great attraction for locals. Jennison added a small collection of birds in another corner of his property and made a modest charge to see his garden and aviary.

The realisation that the public would pay to see something different sparked Jennison's imagination. Although he was only a part-time gardener with an interest in wildlife, he had the vision and determination to make things happen. As he added to his aviary, he had much bigger plans in mind for the people of Manchester. He didn't so much want them to see the world, he wanted to bring the world to them. They would travel the globe without ever leaving their home city. If the north of England ever came close to producing a Walt Disney, John Jennison was surely that man. At its peak, Belle Vue attracted two million paying customers a year, had close to two hundred staff and was housed on a 165-acre site. Not a bad progression from a garden zoo at the Jennison residence.

Jennison was born in Bulwell, Nottingham in 1793. The family moved to Macclesfield when John was still a child and his father, a successful businessman, built a house in Adswood, Stockport on a half-acre plot. Jennison junior had a passion for nature, and botany in particular, but he followed his father into the silk business before inheriting the family home in 1825. He had taken a job as a gardener as the pull of nature refused to let go and following a spell at Lawson's Pleasure Gardens, he became enraptured by the delight a small collection of animals brought to its patrons.

Jennison's own garden on Adswood Lane was, as you might imagine, beautifully laid out and his collection of birds was an added attraction. So it was that in 1826, assisted by his wife, he opened the garden to the public, calling it Strawberry Gardens. While his wife sold home-grown fruit and vegetables – her strawberries were said to be delicious – Jennison continued to add to his small collection of animals. Such was the success of their little venture that, within five years, it was a full-time business.

The demand to see the gardens and zoo was nothing short of incredible and the couple also transformed their home into a brew house, which proved equally successful. Manchester was growing fast and there was a huge void waiting to be filled in terms of the demand for high-quality entertainment. Jennison was the perfect man to fill it.

His ingenuity had attracted the attention of several wealthy businessmen and one, George Gill, strongly encouraged the Stockport entrepreneur to expand. Gill suggested a thirty-six-acre site just off the new road from Hyde to Manchester.

Jennison, who thought highly of Gill, went to have a look and could see the possibilities as he walked around the plot, his mind running wild with ideas. He wasted no time in pursuing his dream and took out a mortgage for £300, which covered the cost of a six-month lease on Belle Vue and also paid off the £80 owing on Strawberry Gardens, which would stay open for the time being. With their belongings crammed onto a handcart and three birdcages and assorted birds, the Jennisons made the seven-mile journey from Adswood and took up permanent residence at Belle Vue. Once in situ, Jennison's imagination caught fire. Within six months he had entered into a contract to lease the land for ninety-nine years, winding down the operation in Adswood. The sheer scale of his plan caused cynics to forecast it would never happen. It was too grand, too exotic, too far-fetched; but not for John Jennison.

The land at Belle Vue was far from ideal. There was much work to be done and a further mortgage, of £800, was taken out to fund the improvements. Extensive lime digging had taken place over a period of time and a series of small waterways criss-crossed certain areas where shipments had been taken to kilns by boat. Some had been filled in, but a number of long, narrow ponds remained. The ground was marshy and unsuitable for any number of activities. Jennison appreciated his project might take years to come to fruition and also that his dreams could sink into the boggy ground that plagued the site.

Although Belle Vue opened for business in 1836 the early years were difficult. The size of the project meant he needed alternative entrances other than Hyde Road and so he drew up plans to have another gate on Stockport Road, which was a far busier route to the city and toll-free, but again this would take time and money. The failure to sell his home in Adswood was also holding up his plans and he enjoyed only moderate success with his gardens and small animal collection in the early years. Worse still, he faced competition from the Manchester Zoological Gardens in Higher Broughton, which housed a far more impressive collection of animals, reptiles and birds. Then when the

Manchester and Birmingham Railway sliced through part of his land, he had to shelve plans for the alternative entrance on Stockport Road. Jennison faced a fight to save his dream, one he was more than willing to take on, but his destiny was taken out of his own hands when an economic downturn led to a dramatic drop in admissions. Turnover fell away and his creditors, tired of waiting for the grand plans to bear fruit, lost patience and began bankruptcy proceedings.

In 1843, the land was put up for sale, but Jennison, far from being deterred, borrowed more money, which enabled him to pay off his most persistent creditors. Another businessman who was owed money accepted beer brewed at Belle Vue in lieu of his cash. Suitably impressed by his resilience, the remaining creditors came to the conclusion that the only way they would ever see a return on their investment was to let Jennison get on with it. With animals from the now-defunct Higher Broughton Zoo added to his own collection, Jennison had fresh impetus and no rivals to worry about. The creation of a train station at Longsight at last meant an alternative entrance to the grounds could be provided. The rail link proved to be a godsend, with trains offering cheap deals for the park. Belle Vue, once again, was on its way.

Even in those early years the delights of Belle Vue were many and varied. There were gardens, a zoo, a maze, a natural-history museum, a ballroom and a great lake with two paddle-steamers. But Jennison was always on the lookout for new and exciting attractions for his customers and he would travel far and wide to look at what was on offer elsewhere. One of his most successful innovations was the firework display, an idea he had picked up after attending the Great Exhibition of 1851 in London. This was a spectacle to behold: against a thirty-thousand square foot canvas known as 'The Picture' men would act out battle scenes, while four thousand spectators looked on from a specially built gallery. Another crowd pleaser was the brass-band contest, which started in 1852 and ran for decades. This was genuinely innovative and many believe that brass-band music was effectively invented at Belle Vue.

However, Belle Vue was much more than simply a pleasure garden, if indeed the word simply is appropriate to describe such a grand institution. Jennison wanted the place to be self-sufficient and went a long way to achieving that ambition. Most building work was done in-house using bricks made in Belle Vue's own brickworks. It was no cottage industry and it is recorded that 1.6 million bricks were produced in 1853 alone. Beer, particularly ginger beer, was another speciality and as production ramped up the Jennisons built a brewery on Hyde Road in 1872. Belle Vue staff grew vegetables, made pots and pans, baskets and barrels, indeed anything that saved them buying from outside suppliers. The park had its own gasworks, which not only supplied Belle Vue but also many of the houses in the vicinity.

By the mid-1860s, Jennison, a father of six, had another battle to fight but this time his drive and never-say-attitude could do little to help him. Diagnosed with cancer of the face, he had his nose cut off in a bid to stem the spread of the disease. He was forced to convalesce in Torquay and West Yorkshire and in his absence his five sons and daughter took over the day-to-day running of the business. John Jennison was never to recover from his illness, and, on 20 September 1867, one of Manchester's greatest visionaries passed away. But his legacy lived on through his children, who would have made their father proud with their vision for Belle Vue's future. George Jennison had been John's right-hand man for the best part of twenty years and he took the reins at his dying father's behest. He was a chip off the old block and thanks to his continuing good work the reputation of the park spread far and wide.

It was helped by an acquisition, which, purely by accident, put Belle Vue onto the front pages of every newspaper in Britain. In 1872 the zoo acquired an elephant called Maharajah from Wombwell's Menagerie No. 1 in Edinburgh, for £680. The plan was to transport Maharajah from Edinburgh to Manchester by train but this was abandoned after the elephant destroyed the railway compartment in which it was to travel. Incredibly, it was decided that Maharajah and his trainer, Lorenzo Lawrence, should instead walk the two hundred miles to Manchester, a journey they completed in ten days. The story became a mobile advert for Belle Vue with daily updates in the newspapers to satisfy a fascinated public. The pachyderm was greeted by huge crowds on its long journey south and people waved and cheered as the great beast passed through their town. It was a marketing masterstroke, albeit an accidental one. Lawrence became the zoo's head elephant keeper, and stayed at Belle Vue for over forty years, while Maharajah provided elephant rides for a decade, until his death from pneumonia in 1882. His skeleton was preserved and added to Belle Vue's natural-history museum. And when the museum was decommissioned in 1941, the skeleton, along with other exhibits, was transferred to the Manchester Museum.

George Jennison died in 1878 and continuing the family tradition, his son, also George, took on the mantle of his father and grandfather. New features and attractions soon appeared: the Italian Gardens, the Indian Grotto and the Lakeside Hotel; while penguin, monkey, camel and elephant houses were added to the zoo as well as a pool for sea lions. In fact, by the early 1900s, Belle Vue appeared to have everything, with several rides and attractions added to the amusement park, as well as a roller-skating rink and an athletics ground. There was also a new concert and exhibition venue, the King's Hall. It soon gained a reputation for attracting the big stars of the day.

By 1919, all of John Jennison's sons had died enabling George to assume complete control, but the Great War took its toll on Belle Vue, with the army using it for training and the public only allowed in at weekends. Many of the two hundred staff volunteered for national service and it proved a difficult time for the park and its owners, who were forced to look at other possibilities to raise income. In 1920, discussions were held with Manchester City about an area of Belle Vue becoming the club's new home, but an agreement couldn't be reached. Another team, Manchester Central FC, was formed with ambitious plans to take on the dominance of City and United, but it failed to prosper.

In 1925, the Jennison interest in Belle Vue ended with the sale of the park and the associated businesses, for which the family received £250,000. It was the end of an era but there was no reason that Manchester's favourite day out should suffer as a result. Belle Vue (Manchester) Ltd were the new owners and one of the first innovations from managing director John Henry Iles was a much-expanded amusement park. It featured many crowd-pleasing attractions, such as the Caterpillar, Scenic Railway and a go-kart track. However, the most renowned ride was The Bobs, so-called because it was a shilling for a ticket. The Bobs, an early rollercoaster, dominated the skyline around Belle Vue. It had an eighty-foot drop at an angle of forty-five degrees, a structure that propelled the cars at a speed of a mile a minute, which of course made it essential for the thrill-seeker. Iles also oversaw the building of a speedway arena, home to the famous Belle Vue Aces, which would become one of the most successful teams in the country thanks to riders like Ivan Mauger and Peter Craven.

In 1928 Iles made one of his most momentous, and best, decisions: the conversion of the King's Hall to an auditorium with a central stage, turning it into a concert hall in the round. The new venue flourished and staged concerts, boxing, wrestling and, most importantly of all, the famous Christmas circus. Under ring-master George Lockhart, the circus ran for forty-three years and was a great favourite with the people of Manchester. Lockhart became a local legend and was given the title, Prince of Ringmasters. He was honoured in 1968 when the Christmas circus was renamed the George Lockhart Celebration Circus.

The King's Hall began another famous association in 1941, when the Hallé Orchestra took up residence after its home had been destroyed in the blitz of December 1940. The Hallé would stay for thirty years and during that time the classical fare would be supplemented by many top acts from the world of popular music, among them the Rolling Stones, Led Zeppelin and Bing Crosby.

Following the outbreak of war in September 1939, the forces immediately sequestered the exhibition hall, the restaurants and most of the top floor of the administrative offices. They also took over the sports ground to use as a base for barrage balloons, and dug several air-raid shelters and although the gardens reopened shortly thereafter, parts of the site were requisitioned by Manchester Corporation and converted into allotments to alleviate food shortages. Although the Second World War forced the cancellation of many events, it nevertheless proved lucrative as profits steadily increased and the company made several successful compensation claims for the requisitioning of its facilities. Sadly, one consequence of war was that the special food needed for some of the animals was no longer available and the penguins and sea lions perished as a result.

The immediate post-war period saw record numbers flocking to Belle Vue as people sought out quality entertainment after the privations they had endured during the previous six years. In 1946, following a huge marketing campaign, the park drew quarter of a million visitors over the Easter weekend, with the queues stretching down Hyde Road. A year later an astonishing four hundred thousand patrons attended the 1947 Christmas circus. It seemed that the good times were back, prompting investment from outside sources, including the great showman and holiday-camp owner, Billy Butlin, who also took a seat on the board.

In 1956, the company sold out to Sir Leslie Joseph and his associate Charles Forte. Joseph arrived with a reputation for making grand projects a success and he instantly saw the potential in Belle Vue. The amusement proprietor had earned his reputation for the superb Festival of Britain amusement park and he quickly identified potential improvements. By clearing the centenary gardens away, he could install a water chute and several other attractions. At the same time, the park was given a thorough sprucing up, while the introduction of Louis Tussauds's Waxworks added yet more appeal.

If the accent before had been a mixture of zoo, gardens and entertainment, it was now more focused on entertainment with catering facilities given an upgrade as well as the introduction of several themed restaurants and buffets. That did not mean the zoo was neglected. Going right back to John Jennison, it had always been central to Belle Vue's appeal. There was also great pride in the humane and progressive way the animals were treated. Belle Vue was one of the first zoos to introduce outdoor enclosures and it was also very successful when it came to breeding in captivity.

The zoo was renowned for its wide range of exotic creatures and as well as lions, elephants and giraffes it housed the likes of pythons, kangaroos and oryx (large African antelopes). There were chimps' tea parties, the star of which was Consul, who rode a bike and played the violin. Perhaps the most popular beasts were the tigons, so-called because they were the progeny of male tigers and female lions. In 1936, tigons Kliou (male) and Maude (female) were bought from Dresden zoo and although they were brother and sister they didn't get along and had to be kept in separate enclosures.

Disaster struck Belle Vue on 17 January 1958 when a major fire devastated the great ballroom as what started as a small blaze soon took a strong hold on the wooden structure. By the time the fire brigade arrived it was too late. The total cost of the damage was estimated to be £250,000 and a whole block including ballroom, cafes, shops, bars and the firework viewing stand were lost. Also consumed in the fire was the outdoor dance floor, which was at one time used as a surface for roller skating. Fortunately, thanks to the prompt action of staff and fire-fighters, most of the zoo's animals were saved. The setback couldn't stop the momentum Joseph and Forte had injected and the rebuilding process began almost immediately.

Just as things were beginning to return to normal Belle Vue was hit with another shattering blow. Although it was not on the same scale as the fire of 1958, what happened left the people of Manchester sickened and angry. On 7 April 1960 three teenagers broke into the park and kicked to death two swans, geese, ducks, nine penguins, two pelicans, a Chinese gander and a crowned crane. A number of birds were spared, but seriously injured, and eggs were taken from nests. The attack provoked outrage, with the public demanding the sternest sentences possible. However, the age of the delinquents (12, 13 and 14) meant that little could be done in terms of punishment. The lawyers representing the youths argued that their clients were unlikely to get a fair trial given the hostility towards them and in the end the boys were convicted on five charges and sent to an approved school for three years. The depth of feeling provoked by the bird slaughter proved the affection Mancunians had for Belle Vue and the show of support was a welcome shot in the arm.

In the early 1960s, the great-ape house arrived and the constant improvements meant the crowds continued to flock to Hyde Road. The addition of Dodge City, with a Wild West re-enactment, also proved extremely popular. During the early 1960s, the park could still attract 150,000 visitors on Easter Monday. Revenues were healthy and the catering overhaul proved to be particularly profitable as Joseph had learned what had worked well at the Festival of Britain and utilised that knowledge to great effect. Yet there was to be another change of ownership in 1963 when Charles Forte took over as sole proprietor. Like his predecessors, he was keen to bring in his own ideas as well as utilising his catering organisation further still. Outdoor enclosures for lions and tigers were introduced, as well as wolf wood, while the Palm Court restaurant was turned into Caesar's Palace.

By the late 1960s, however, Forte was swimming against the tide.

Faced with increased competition at home from the likes of Alton Towers, and with the advent of cheap package holidays in the sun, attendances fell at an alarming rate. For the first time, questions were asked about a long-term future for the Showground of the World. One by one, attractions were phased out and shows began to close. Gradually, the appeal faded. The price of oil rose sharply in 1974 making some of the animal houses expensive to heat and, slowly but surely, Belle Vue stuttered towards inevitable closure. Although admissions held their own in the mid-Seventies, the zoo, which was no longer financially viable, closed its doors for the last time on 11 September 1977.

The amusement aspect of the park continued into the next decade, but Belle Vue had become a shadow of its former self. Litter blew in some areas that had been shut down, the paintwork became flecked and discoloured and on colder days it was a dreary, depressing place to visit. The decline was so marked that customers only visited out of a sense of nostalgia. By the start of the 1980s the only option was to sell the land and a deal was thrashed out with developers. They planned housing and businesses where lions and tigers had once roamed, fireworks had lit the night sky and steamers sailed the great lake.

The people of Manchester were aghast that Belle Vue was on the verge of closure and a petition with fifty thousand signatures was presented to Manchester City Council, but to no avail. In October 1980, the greatest show in the north – indeed the world, as far as Mancunians were concerned – shut up shop. The speedway stadium was sold in 1982 and continues to this day, as does the greyhound racing while a cinema, snooker hall and bowling alley remain on the plot. The Kings Hall survived for a few more years before the opening of the G-MEX meant that Manchester probably had one concert hall too many. In 1987, it too gave up the ghost. Since the demise of Belle Vue, Manchester has lacked a real family day out, which is disappointing for a city of this size and importance.

How successful a modern Belle Vue might be today can only be guessed at. One thing is for sure: things have been a lot duller since it closed its doors. The Showground of the World is sorely missed, but to those who can still remember the tingle of excitement as they entered the magical kingdom for the first time, the memories will last a lifetime.

16
CARDUS

The boy from the Manchester slum who became not only the greatest cricket writer of the age, but also the finest classical-music critic. The pupil who left school at twelve, but who astonished the great and the good of English letters with his profound knowledge of the classics. The former insurance clerk who had the nerve to ask the greatest newspaper editor in the land for a job. The illegitimate son of a prostitute who was knighted by the Queen.

It is a rags-to-riches story that even Hollywood would reject as too far-fetched.

Or is it?

There is no disputing either Neville Cardus's virtuosity or his originality as a journalist and author. Many good judges argue that he invented modern cricket reporting; Cardus, they insist, didn't change the rules of sports journalism, he wrote new ones. Yet his life is shrouded in conjecture and myth, much of it created by the man himself as he reshaped his past to suit the requirements of the present.

Even the circumstances of his birth are unclear. He came into the world on 2 April 1889, the son of Ada Cardus, and was christened John Frederick Neville Cardus although as his birth was never registered we only have his mother's word for it. Cardus was his mother's maiden name and the fact is that his true paternity will never be known. In his autobiography (published in 1947), Cardus writes that his father was 'tall, saturnine of countenance and one of the first violins in an orchestra'. In order to satisfy the strict morals of the time, a story was put around that the 'first violinist' had gone to West Africa on business where he subsequently died. This may or may not be true and Cardus never made clear to anyone if he knew the true identity of his father. Another possibility, given that Ada was a prostitute, is that no one knew for certain.

For his part Cardus always insisted that he never believed the story about his father going to Africa. On his wedding certificate he gave the name of his father as Frederick Cardus, occupation civil servant, but then, in 1951, for his entry in *Who's Who*, he describes himself as the son of Robert Stanislaw Cardus and Ada Newsome (Newsome being the surname of one of his mother's many consorts). Not that he was ever embarrassed by his origins; in later life he used it as a conversational gambit to amuse his friends.

Given her circumstances Ada had no alternative but to turn to her family for support after the birth of her child. She and little Fred (as Neville was then known) lived with her father, Robert Cardus, and mother, Ann Cardus, at 4 Summer Place in Rusholme. The full, extended Cardus family resided there under one roof, including Ada's two sisters Beatrice and Jessica.

Neville Cardus always gave the impression he was brought up in the midst of squalor. 'Manchester was my place of birth, in a slum,' he notes in his autobiography. In fact, it was nothing of the sort. Christopher Brookes has written an excellent biography of Cardus (*His Own Man: The Life of Neville Cardus*, published in 1985) and in that book he makes the point that the Rusholme his subject grew up in was 'at the centre of a bustling, colourful cosmopolitan community. Artisans, teachers, clerks and constables lived side by side with families displaced by one or other of those tides of human migration which spread European stock to all parts of the globe.'

Nor by any means was the Cardus residence in Summer Place a hovel. It was well appointed, at least by the standards of the day. There was a lounge with a bay window and the dwelling also boasted a toilet, even if it was in the back yard. The toilet was admittedly a pail closet but this was common at the time and infinitely superior to the sanitary arrangements of the real Manchester slums. In later life it clearly suited Cardus to exaggerate the circumstances of his youth, much as he chose to romanticise the character of his mysterious father.

It is impossible to judge the influence of his mother Ada on young Fred as he grew up. There are few references to her in his series of autobiographical works, despite the fact that she died as late as 1954 having lived to a ripe old age. According to some accounts this was because she preferred to entertain her clients away from the city and was therefore absent for long periods. In fact anyone reading Cardus's books and newspaper columns would glean very little about his nearest and dearest.

There is only one exception to his reticence on family matters: his aunt, Beatrice. To say that she was a colourful character is something of an understatement. A tall, striking woman with intense blue eyes, dressed in the latest fashions from Paris, she was able to put her considerable feminine attributes to work in the loucher parts of Manchester. Aunt Beatrice was a prostitute and a very successful one at that. The young Fred adored her, and she him. She was the mother he never really knew, someone he turned to for guidance and love. It was Beatrice who sang him to sleep at night, it was Beatrice who encouraged him to read good books, and, most importantly, it was Beatrice who gave him his first cricket bat.

Not that the boy had any illusions about his aunt's profession. He saw only too clearly her preparations for work: the heavy make-up; the cheap but alluring perfume; the gaudy dresses. He saw too the string of men who knocked furtively on the door of 4 Summer Place, before being quickly ushered up the stairs to Beatrice's boudoir. In his autobiography he vividly describes one such encounter: 'One night I entered the house and found two broker's men ensconced in the little living room. My aunt explained to me that she had run into debt. She sent me out of the house. "Go and read in the library." When I came home again fairly late the broker's men had gone.' Neville's reward for cooperating was a crisp ten-shilling note, handed to him the next morning by his grateful aunt.

However, Beatrice was to make a much bigger impression on her young nephew – and indeed on the city of Manchester – with an outrageous lawsuit. In 1902, during one of her regular trawls for customers in the many pubs, clubs and restaurants of the city centre she met Mustapha Karsa, the Turkish consul and a wealthy businessman. A passionate affair ensued and the couple moved between luxury hotels in Blackpool, Southport and Liverpool, scandalising respectable opinion in both Manchester and Sale, where the married Karsa lived.

Inevitably, the Turk's interest waned and he rejected her. Beatrice, however, was a fighter and she brought an action for breach of promise at Manchester assizes. The press went to town, devoting many column inches to the affair of the 'Lustful Turk' and the good-time girl from Rusholme. It is highly unlikely that Karsa had any intention of plight-ing his troth – not with a wife and eight children at home – but he may have led her on.

In court the Cardus family trooped through the dock, testifying that the Turk had indeed promised marriage. Juicy titbits emerged, including details of the fine clothes and jewellery he had bought her. The packed gallery also heard a 'scandalous' account of a night they spent in a Liverpool hotel, where, to gasps and titters, it was revealed that 'they occupied the same bedroom'. Beatrice was fortunate that the judge, Mr Justice Wills, thought little either of Mustapha Karsa or his defence. She also used her feminine charm on Judge Wills, as Neville explains in his autobiography: 'As soon as Beatrice went into the box she attempted to prejudice or corrupt the judge with a smile. The judge throughout the hearing was on her side obviously, and who wouldn't have been?' When both sides had presented their evidence, Wills summed-up for the jury. No one in the courtroom could have any doubt that he clearly favoured Beatrice's version of events. The jury agreed and awarded her £200 in damages, a not inconsiderable sum for the time.

It is hardly surprising that a colourful character like Aunt Beatrice features heavily in Neville Cardus's autobiographical works and it is perhaps at the expense of hard facts about his childhood. One thing we do know is that he played cricket whenever he could, on any patch of vacant ground he could find, and became a fine spin bowler, much in demand from teams in the lower leagues of Lancashire cricket. When he found the time he made his way to Old Trafford, home of Lancashire cricket, where a lifelong love affair with his home county was born. His youthful imagination was fired by the excellent sides that Lancashire then produced and two characters in particular stood out: Archibald Campbell MacLaren and Reginald Herbert Spooner. MacLaren, the former captain of Harrow, made his Lancashire debut in 1890 and became a county legend. A master batsman, A. C. was also a great cricket tactician and captained both Lancashire and England with great authority.

While Cardus was in awe of MacLaren, he considered Spooner an immortal. Like his captain Spooner was a former public schoolboy, and he displayed effortless superiority on the cricket pitch (and also as a three-quarter on the rugby field, in which capacity he was capped by England). He cut a tall, elegant figure and was the batting stylist par excellence, punishing bowlers at domestic and international levels with the full array of classic shots. As Cardus would later write, 'His strokes would have honoured the lawns of a royal palace.' He hero-worshipped Spooner, copied his hairstyle and would wander the streets inconsolable on the rare occasions that the great man failed to score.

The young Cardus attended a Board (or council) school in Grove Street, where the elementary education he received was supplemented by long sessions in Manchester's many local libraries, especially the one on Dickenson Road. Manchester, though an industrial city, was deeply cultural. As one of his contemporaries later noted, 'There are few communities in the world which are more emphatically reading communities than Manchester . . . its literary institutions are numerous, and possessed of extensive libraries.'

Cardus took full advantage of Manchester's obsession with books. His tastes were elevated. He devoured Dickens, Thackeray and Hardy, as well as the great philosophers. He would walk for miles to attend lectures at the Islington Hall, Ancoats, where the likes of George Bernard Shaw addressed the great issues of the day. Music too was an important part of his life. There were many music halls in the city, which he gladly attended, but his tastes became more rarefied and he was soon a regular at the classical concerts given at the Royal Manchester College of Music. The young Cardus was the archetypal autodidact, or self-educated man.

It was around this time that he decided to ditch the Fred moniker and to adopt Neville, a more appropriate name for someone determined to better himself. It certainly did him no harm when he applied for the job that would change his life. In early 1912 he noticed an advert for the post of assistant professional at Shrewsbury, a leading public school.

Thanks mainly to his prowess as a local-league cricketer he got the position. It turned out to be the perfect billet: long hot summers on the playing fields; plenty of time to devote to reading and writing; an inspirational father figure in the form of headmaster Dr Cyril Alington.

In his writings, Cardus often gives the impression that his great success was down to a combination of luck and destiny. Nothing could be further from the truth. He was fiercely ambitious and to improve his literary skills he would copy out substantial extracts from the classics in longhand. It was his unique way of immersing himself in words. And it was with words that he wanted to work. After he left Shrewsbury in the late summer of 1916 he returned to Manchester as an unemployed man of twenty-seven. By this time he had no doubt about what he wanted to do. He was desperate to become a journalist and not just with any old rag. He set his sights on the paper that was then the most prestigious in England: the *Manchester Guardian*.

Founded in 1821 by Manchester cotton merchant John Edward Taylor, the *Guardian*'s golden years date from 1872 when Taylor's nephew, Charles Prestwich (C. P.) Scott, became the editor (he bought the paper in 1907). Scott, a fearless campaigner, gave the paper a much more radical tone, supporting many controversial causes, such as women's suffrage and opposition to the Boer War. As a former Liberal MP and president of the Manchester Liberal Federation he was highly influential in political and journalistic circles. But it was as a newspaperman that he is remembered, making the *Guardian* a respected voice at home and abroad during his astonishing fifty-seven years in the editor's chair. He also coined one of journalism's most famous phrases when, in an article celebrating the paper's centenary, he wrote with typical high-mindedness that, 'Comment is free, but facts are sacred.'

Little wonder that Neville Cardus was so keen to join such a news-paper and such an editor, and so entranced was he by the *Guardian* that he would spend many hours hanging around its premises in Cross Street, pining for the opportunity to be part of it. He could procrastinate no longer and in January 1917 he wrote to Scott, asking if there was any work he could do there, whether as a proof-reader or in the general office. He enclosed two essays: one on music; the other on philosophy. Scott must have seen something in the young man's writings because he invited him to his grand house, the Firs, in Fallowfield, for an interview. Cardus was offered a job all right, but as secretary to Scott and his place of work was to be the Firs, not Cross Street. After a month working without pay, Scott dismissed him. He had come tantalisingly close to his dream but now his hopes had been dashed.

Cardus needn't have worried. A few months later he was invited for interview again, this time as a reporter, and he was delighted to accept Scott's second offer of employment. Assigned to the reporter's room, he rubbed shoulders with some of the greatest journalists in the world. At the time he had no ambition to be a sports writer, much less a cricket correspondent. The truth is that the greatest cricket writer in history was introduced to writing about the game purely by chance. In fact chance does not cover it; divine intervention would be closer to the truth.

In 1919 after a serious pulmonary condition had left Cardus bed-ridden for two months the *Manchester Guardian*'s news editor, W. P. Crozier, suggested he should convalesce in the sun by attending the cricket at Old Trafford. It would be better for him than his usual beat on the arts pages. Perhaps, the news editor suggested, he might care to cover a few matches while he was there.

The rest is history.

Cricket reporting at that time consisted of little more than listing the bare facts: runs scored, wickets taken, rain stops play. That would never be enough for Neville Cardus. Although his first few pieces were rejected on the grounds of long-windedness, C. P. Scott saw the angel in the marble and gave strict instructions that his copy was to be published in full. Cardus for his part was, at best, ambivalent. He was grateful for the work but did not feel that writing on a subject like cricket was up to his lofty intellectual standards. If he was on the horns of a dilemma, it was solved in 1920 when Scott offered him a permanent position as cricket correspondent on very attractive terms.

A name had to be found for the new man's reports, or, to put it in newspaper parlance, a by-line. Neville was still producing reviews and features for the arts pages of the *Guardian* and in order to distinguish this output from the cricket articles the paper had to come up with an appropriate by-line. After much head scratching, it was news editor Crozier's secretary who christened the column, Cricketer. It was simple, yet entirely appropriate, and soon readers were lapping up his dispatches. By 1922 the summer readership of the paper had doubled, thanks to cricket followers anxious to read Cardus's account of the goings-on at Old Trafford. Within just five years he was recognised as the sports writer par excellence.

What was it that made his writing on the game so special? Cardus's genius was to invest the cricketers he watched with the full range of human emotions, linking them from the cricket pitch to the wider world and beyond. To him, they were characters from English literature, heroes from Classical mythology or the tragic figures of grand opera. In this extract he describes with typical wit how certain legendary players wielded their bats.

> A bat, indeed, can look an entirely different instrument in different hands. With Grace it was a rod of correction, for to him bad bowling was a deviation from moral order; Ranjitsinhji turned a bat into a wand, passing it before the eyes of the foe till they followed him in a trance along his processional way; George Hirst's bat looked like a stout cudgel belabouring all men not born in Yorkshire; Macartney used his bat for bedazzlement, as Sergeant Troy used his blade for the bedazzlement of Bathsheba – it was a bat that seemed everywhere at once, yet nowhere specially.

That extract with its allusions to Troy and Bathsheba, characters in Thomas Hardy's novel *Far from the Madding Crowd*, perfectly illustrates the ease with which he wove literary references into his writing, as well as his vivid imagination and elegant style. However, he was also an astute observer of the game and could analyse a player's strengths and weaknesses as well as anyone. Here he is on Wilfred Rhodes, the great Yorkshire and England all-rounder, in a piece penned in 1928.

> Rhodes gets his men out before the ball pitches; spin with him is an accessory after the act of flight – flight which disguises the ball's length, draws the batsman forward when he ought to play back, sends him playing back when he ought to come forward, and generally keeps him in a state of mind so confused that in time he feels it might be a mercy to get out. Against Rhodes, no long innings has ever been played that did not at the end find the batsman intellectually a little worn and weary.

Cardus worshipped great cricketers, even when they were destroying his beloved Lancashire or England. It seemed that the greater the feat, the more eloquent his response. A good example is his attitude to the great Donald Bradman, who arrived for his first Ashes series in England in 1930. After Bradman had scored 254 at Lord's, 334 at Headingley (then the highest Test score ever) and 232 at the Oval, Cardus was moved to write a wonderful 'Appreciation', from which this extract is taken.

> Perhaps he is marked off from the greatest of his predecessors not so much by technique as by temperament . . . a hundred runs is nothing to him; he conceives his innings in terms which go far beyond Trumper's or Macartney's most avaricious dreams. He has demonstrated that a batsman can hit forty-two boundaries in a day without once giving the outfielders hope of a catch; he has kindled grand bonfires of batsmanship for us. But never once has he burned his own fingers while lighting them.

Bradman recognised a fellow genius when he saw one. He described the Mancunian as 'the best of all writers in the cricket world' and the two men became firm friends, a friendship that was cemented during the seven years that Cardus spent in Australia from 1940 to 1947.

While he fully merited his success Cardus, it has to be said, was also in the right place at the right time. During the interwar years, Lancashire Cricket Club had a succession of formidable elevens. Ernest Tyldesley of Worsley – Lancashire's top run scorer of all time – was a marvellous batsman and was ably supported by his older brother, Johnny. The team could also call on the services of two other batting greats: Harry 'Old Shake' Makepeace and Charlie Hallows. While in the early days the Lancashire bowling might not have been as formidable, it was immeasurably strengthened by the arrival at Old Trafford of two county legends in Ted McDonald and Cecil Parkin, along with a wicket keeper par excellence in George Duckworth.

Cardus had a special relationship with Cecil Parkin. Parkin was much more than a cricketer. He was a joker and something of an oddball, keeping his teammates amused during rain delays with his conjuring tricks and practical jokes, and he gave the reporters great copy with his often outspoken criticism of the cricket authorities. Voted *Wisden* cricketer of the year in 1924, Parkin then helped Lancashire win its first county championship for two decades in 1926. While other writers frowned on Parkin's antics – arguing that he was too often interested in playing to the gallery than in getting opposition batsmen out – Cardus recognised his true worth, not only as cricketer but also as an entertainer. In this perceptive piece, appropriately entitled 'Parkin – the Card', he sums him up perfectly.

> He won a lot of handsome names – *l'enfant terrible* of cricket, the Artful Dodger, the Merry Andrew, the Jack Ketch of cricket. He deserved them all, and, because of that, he never lacked judges. 'With what great cause was he ever identified?' ask the guardians of law and order . . . We can surely respond with the answer that was triumphantly given on behalf of 'The Card': 'Why, with the great cause of cheering us all up?'

Parkin and his colleagues helped Lancashire to win five county champion-ships in those glorious interwar years, a haul only bettered by their bitter rivals from across the Pennines, Yorkshire. It was the perfect scenario for a man of Cardus's abilities: an outstanding 'home' team full of larger-than-life characters and all-consuming rivalry with their nearest neighbours. Many have observed that had Neville Cardus's beat been Leicester or Northampton he would not have enjoyed the same success. That is almost certainly true: few counties had either the mystique or traditions of Lancashire; nor did they play their home matches at one of the most famous cricket grounds in the world.

A prolific journalist like Cardus needed big characters and prolific he certainly was, turning in nine thousand words a week to Cross Street. It would not be long before publishers expressed an interest in collect-ing the best of his writings. His first tome, *A Cricketer's Book*, appeared as early as 1922, and was quickly followed by a several more in the same vein. With the royalties from his books and a steady salary from his day job, Cardus, perhaps for the first time in his life, had money in the bank.

That relative prosperity had enabled him to make a big change in his personal life. He got married. Neville had known Edith King, a schoolteacher from Victoria Park, since his days at Shrewsbury. By day Edith taught at the Ducie Avenue Central School for Girls and by night she threw herself into a wide range of artistic activities, including painting and avant-garde theatre. Perhaps it was the artistic temperament that allowed her to be so understanding about her husband's absences and his penchant for the ladies. Despite the couple owning a house in Withington, they were apart as often as they were together, with Neville making frequent trips to London on *Guardian* business, where he stayed at the National Liberal Club.

A flourishing career, a healthy income, the respect of his peers, the appreciation of his readers and an understanding wife: life for Neville Cardus was sweet. Then, in 1927, it got even sweeter.

In May of that year, Samuel Langford, the *Manchester Guardian*'s respected music critic, died. It was a job that Cardus yearned for, and he had been encouraged in his ambition by none other than C. P. Scott. The great editor, impressed by a piece Cardus had written while on the paper's arts desk, advised his protégé to expand his knowledge of classical music. Cardus didn't need to be told twice: as Christopher Brookes points out in his biography, the years leading up to Cardus's appointment as Langford's successor 'marked the culmination of a period of preparation in which he [Cardus] had studied music as diligently as ever Leonardo had studied anatomy'.

As in so many other fields, Manchester was then a centre of excellence for music. Sir Thomas Beecham had raised the standard of the Hallé Orchestra to new heights and musical greats from around the world – including Richard Strauss – flocked to the Free Trade Hall to take their place on the podium as guest conductors. By the time Cardus arrived on the scene, the Hallé's principal conductor was Hamilton Harty, regarded by some as a genius but by others as overly conservative in his choice of repertoire. Cardus was in the second camp. He wrote many critical reviews of Harty's concerts and that criticism extended to the orchestra's players, many of whom resented Cardus's comments at a time when the Hallé was struggling to attract audiences in a time of great economic hardship. It was not that he was being critical for the sake of being critical; it was out of concern for a great institution, one that he had huge affection for. He had grown up with the Hallé and was keen for it to return to what he saw as its glory days.

By now the musical world was Cardus's oyster. While still a regular at the Free Trade Hall, he was more and more drawn to the bright lights and thriving cultural scene in London. With his reputation as a music critic in the ascendant, he enjoyed the friendship of the great and the good, dining out regularly with the capital's cultural elite. They included the great playwright, J. M. Barrie, the author of *Peter Pan*, novelist and playwright J. B. Priestley and conductor and impresario Sir Thomas Beecham.

Those trips to London were about more than journalism or even socialising with famous friends. In the autumn of 1928 he met the woman who would become the great passion of his life, at least for the eight years their affair lasted. Her name was Hilda Elizabeth Ede, or as she was known to her friends and family, Barbe. According to Cardus he first set eyes on Barbe at Charing Cross Station, where he noticed her laddered stocking, which gave him a sexual thrill the like of which he had never experienced. Voluptuous, worldly and pushy, Barbe enchanted Cardus. She was equally smitten. Her husband, a banker, was staid and a home bird, quite the opposite of the talkative and sociable journalist.

Such was his devotion to Barbe that he even rented a small flat in Victoria, where they enjoyed regular trysts. Despite his delight in the affair he agonised about his disloyalty to Edith, and thought seriously about confessing everything to her. In the end, at a dinner in Manchester's Midland Hotel, he told his wife the whole sorry saga. Edith wasn't surprised; nor was she angry. She accepted Neville, warts and all, and her understanding nature allowed them to have almost half a century of marital bliss, even if it was of the rather unconventional kind. As she told a friend: 'Ee, I like him to have his little girls. It makes him so much better tempered when he comes home. He doesn't know I know, but I do.'

An agreeable job, an attractive mistress, the delights of London – and an understanding wife two hundred miles away in Manchester. What more could one ask for? But it was all about to come to a shuddering halt. The reason? Adolf Hitler. The start of the Second World War in September 1939 changed the lives of everyone in Britain and Neville Cardus was no exception. Cultural life was much diminished, professional cricket shut down and many journalists found themselves at a considerable loose end. Cardus was one of them. He felt useless, almost unemployed.

Help, however, was at hand.

In December 1939, he received a telegram from the great Australian newspaper proprietor Sir Keith Murdoch (father of Rupert) inviting him to cover a musical tour being led by Sir Thomas Beecham for the *Melbourne Herald*. He didn't need to be asked twice. Within weeks he was down under, working for six months in Melbourne before moving six months later to Sydney, Australia's largest city, to write for the *Sydney Morning Herald*, where he would stay for six years. The move caused a few eyebrows to be raised at home. Britain, after all, was fighting for her very survival against a ruthless enemy and although Cardus was in his fifties when he left, and therefore too old to fight, some took the view that he was deserting a sinking ship. It has even been suggested that his decision to leave England was the reason that he was never granted the freedom of the city of Manchester. The criticism of his move to Australia is perhaps a little unfair: after all he had volunteered to serve in the First World War, being rejected on the grounds of ill health.

On his return to England in 1946, Cardus continued in the journalistic profession, in the first instance with the *Evening Standard*, and latterly with his old paper, the *Manchester Guardian*, where he accepted the post of London music critic and a roving brief to cover the biggest cricket matches. Although he was inevitably less prolific than in his pre-war heyday, he still turned out highly regarded reviews of concerts put on by the capital's many resident orchestras and guest performers, with the occasional cricket piece thrown in for good measure.

If his output had diminished, the regard in which he was held had not. A second volume of autobiography appeared in 1950: entitled *Second Innings* it caught the imagination of critics and public alike. The great poet Siegfried Sassoon wrote to him, lavishly praising the book and noting that, 'the writing . . . makes me, as one autobiographer to another, glow with satisfaction'. Then, in 1959, he achieved one of his greatest ambitions when he was accepted as a member of the Garrick, the grandest of London's gentleman's clubs. There was also an invitation to appear as the castaway on *Desert Island Discs*. Official recognition followed. In 1964 he was appointed CBE and then, in the 1967 New Year's Honours List, he was knighted, the first twentieth-century music critic to be so honoured.

These accolades delighted Cardus. Yet it was two accolades from his home city of Manchester that gratified him above all others. In 1966, to mark his fifty years with the *Guardian*, the Hallé orchestra put on two concerts in his honour, the first in Manchester and the other in London. There was however one sour note: after making a speech congratulating Cardus, conductor Sir John Barbirolli had been asked to make a presentation to him on behalf of the *Guardian*. But when Cardus opened the envelope he pulled out a cheque, to the value of £100. It was an incredibly mean gesture for a man who had done so much for the reputation and circulation of the paper. Although Cardus maintained a dignified silence in the Free Trade Hall, he later complained bitterly to friends about the '£2 for every year I worked for them'. He had always felt undervalued by the paper's management and this confirmed their parsimony.

The second honour occasioned only pure joy. In 1971 he was invited to become the President of the Lancashire Cricket Club. He gratefully accepted and from that day on was an enthusiastic and conscientious father figure for the club. The boy who had watched legends like MacLaren and Spooner, and as a young reporter, Parkin and Tyldesley, was now presiding over its affairs.

The only sadness was that Edith was not there to see it. She passed away in 1968, following a heart attack. Despite their unconventional relationship there is no doubt that Sir Neville had great affection for his wife: 'a great and loyal companion,' was how he described her. It left a huge void, and despite a wide circle of friends he was often lonely. Age inevitably meant that he was much less prolific than before and increasingly he felt out of touch with the modern world, and in particular with the *Guardian*, with whose managers and editors he had a series of spats. Sir Neville Cardus died in his sleep on 28 February 1975, at the age of eighty-six.

Cardus revolutionised the world of sports journalism and his influence is still felt today. He was also an eminent music critic, frank and fearless and full of enthusiasm. Yet he never forgot his upbringing in Manchester and at the end of his life, his thoughts would often drift back there: to Aunt Beatrice, a sinner, but the sinner who helped make him the man he was; to Old Trafford on a sunny afternoon as those twin deities

MacLaren and Spooner marched to the crease; to the Free Trade Hall, with the Hallé in its pomp; to the *Manchester Guardian*'s Cross Street offices, presided over by that benevolent dictator C. P. Scott.

17

THE IRK VALLEY RAIL DISASTER

Lying barely two miles north-east of Manchester city centre, Collyhurst is a tough, unforgiving sort of place. It has been home to a disproportionate number of famous residents including Les Dawson, Brian Kidd, Nobby Stiles, Stan Bowles, plus boxers Pat Barrett, Michael Gomez, Johnny King, Jackie Brown and *Love Thy Neighbour* actor Jack Smethurst, all of whom it could be argued had to fight their way to the top. There is an edge and a tangible energy in the air, which is no doubt why the Electric Circus club was at the epicentre of the punk movement in 1970s Manchester; when Collyhurst realised nobody else was interested, it filled the gap.

Bordered by Monsall, Newton Heath, Ancoats and Bradford, Collyhurst is peppered with high-rise flats, terraced housing and council houses and has been described as one of the most deprived areas in Britain. Some will say nothing remarkable ever happens there; the problems with youth crime are well-documented and there is little or no investment. Yet, in 1953, the eyes of the nation were fixed on Collyhurst when it was the locus for a horrendous rail disaster. Two trains collided virtually head on at the Irk Valley junction on the approach to Victoria Station. Later, when investigations had been completed, it emerged that had one of the trains left just five seconds earlier, ten people would not have lost their lives.

The morning of Saturday, 15 August 1953 was typically overcast, with Manchester's leaden skies doing their best to keep summer at bay. It was cool with a light breeze as the 7.20 from Bury to Victoria Station set off. There were around a hundred passengers on board, many fewer than would have been the case on a weekday. The majority were heading into the city to catch connecting trains to London, the Lake District, Wales and the south-west. Railway guard Albert Almond, his wife and teenage daughter had been looking forward to the journey for several weeks, with a train to Devon waiting at Victoria and the promise of a well-earned holiday by the sea. A family from Crumpsall – Margaret Halls, her husband and their 6-year-old son, Jeremy – were on their way to a break on the south coast, excited by the prospect of a first trip to the seaside. The Bury train, built in 1914, was powered by electricity and had five carriages. It seemed that the passengers were in good hands, with Albert Hardman at the controls. Hardman, a former mayor of Bury, was just a few months from retirement having been with the railways for almost fifty years. There were few more experienced drivers anywhere in the country.

Carriage serviceman Ben Edwards, of Whitley Street in Collyhurst, was making his way to work, bleary-eyed and not overly pleased to have an early-Saturday-morning shift ahead of him. He was approaching the Cheetham Hill and Queens Road sidings, around a hundred yards from the Smedley Road viaduct, which traverses the river Irk and the valley below. He had no reason to expect anything out of the ordinary, yet he was about to become a crucial witness to something he would never forget, no matter how hard he tried.

As the Bury train sped towards Victoria, Albert Almond and his family, in the leading and most densely packed carriage, began to take down their luggage from the overhead stow in preparation for arrival. Others followed suit, eager to continue their onward journeys. Meanwhile, the 7.36 steam-engine-led service to Bacup was setting off from Victoria with a smattering of passengers, six in all, heading for the small Lancashire town.

The tracks to and from Victoria run in parallel across the viaduct, but cross at one point. To allow safe negotiation, signals were in place to ensure trains passed a good distance apart. However, on this occasion, a series of human errors saw long-standing procedures ignored. As the steam train approached the viaduct, the signal indicated 'danger', but as it slowed and all-but came to a halt, the signal changed to 'off', and so the driver, Fred Heap, proceeded with caution across the viaduct at six miles per hour, slowly gathering momentum.

Signalman Arthur Clayton, 25, had overslept that morning, arriving for his five o'clock shift almost an hour-and-a-half late. He would later wish he'd missed it entirely as he became central to what was to follow. Having allowed the steam engine to cross the viaduct, he became concerned about the whereabouts of the Bury train, which he assumed was yet to pass the last station before Victoria at Woodlands Road, a good few minutes away. Normal procedure would have been to get confirmation that the 7.20 was either at, or approaching, Woodlands Road.

Concerned that he didn't know its precise whereabouts, Clayton called William Upton at the Woodlands Road signal box to enquire where the Bury train was. Upton said he would contact the controlling officer and find out. But he didn't get the chance to enquire because he saw the train from Bury speeding past. Knowing that a collision was inevitable he uttered the chilling words, 'It's passing here now!'

Clayton looked up to see the trains hurtling towards each other. Helplessly, he looked on, knowing that disaster was about to strike. At 7.40, the locomotives met at the Irk Valley junction, smashing into each other in a head-on collision. Steam-engine driver Heap would later admit he thought his train had simply been derailed. 'I never saw the electric train at all,' he later told the inquest. He wasn't alone. It later emerged that the whereabouts of the Bury train had been a mystery to two of the signalmen. It had, in fact, been 'lost' for several minutes.

The leading carriage of the electric train took the full brunt of the crash, smashing through a parapet wall on the viaduct. As the carriages behind impacted, it was pushed off and over the edge of the viaduct, where, in mid-air, it agonisingly held on to its couplings for a few seconds before dropping ninety feet into the Irk and the steep bank below. The leading carriage of the steam engine crashed into the parapet on the other side of the viaduct, sustaining substantial damage, but the wall withstood the impact. As there were houses directly below the viaduct on that side, the loss of life could have been considerable if the wall had been breached.

Railwayman Edwards, who was now very close to the viaduct, saw a blue flash at the point of impact and the carriage crash through the wall and over the edge. He recalled watching as it hung momentarily in mid-air during which time he heard 'things inside falling to the bottom of the carriage' before the sickening plunge.

The river was only waist deep but it still submerged part of the stricken carriage where most of the casualties lay, many already dead. Among those who survived the crash, but were now in danger of drowning, was 6-year-old Jeremy Halls who had slipped beneath the water. Even fifty years on from the accident, he recalled the moment vividly.

> I did see the steam engine coming the other way and have a strong memory of seeing flying glass. Split seconds later I remember thrashing about under the water. People were tumbling down to the bottom of the coach. Then I was dragged to safety by a youth who saved me from drowning and I owe my life to him.

The alarm was raised immediately by Edwards and the emergency services were soon in attendance. For Bury train driver, Albert Hardman, just weeks from retirement, there was nothing that could be done. He had died instantly, on impact, and his broken body lay near the collision point. By contrast the crew of the sturdier, 88-tonne steam engine escaped without injury and were able to jump clear of their stricken engine, which had been pushed onto its side.

Doctors, nurses, police and firemen with acetylene cutting equipment were on the scene within ten minutes and were soon treating the injured. The main focus was the submerged portion of the carriage, with many victims trapped in the wreckage. Some people would escape with minor injuries, while twenty-two were seriously injured. For others, nothing could be done: seven bodies were recovered, plus Albert Hardman's, and two people died on the way to hospital.

Little Jeremy Halls escaped with just a few bruises but his mother and father were critically injured. Margaret Halls, 42, died of her injuries on the way to hospital while her husband suffered a broken back. Having lost his mother, Jeremy joined his father in hospital as he recovered from chest and spinal injuries. 'We were all absolutely grief stricken,' he said. 'I was carted off to hospital and stayed there for two to three weeks, while my father recovered.'

An inquiry into what caused the accident was quickly convened. One crucial question had to be addressed: how could things have gone so tragically wrong when so many safety procedures were in place? With ten dead and fifty-eight injured, the need for answers was urgent.

However, for those expecting mechanical failure to be the cause the findings were disturbing. It was revealed that signalman Clayton and driver Hardman were responsible for several inexplicable oversights. Clayton's decision to allow the steam engine to go across the viaduct was the start of a chain of critical errors: believing the Bury train to be a safe distance away, he changed the signal from danger and allowed the steam engine to proceed because, as he later explained, he didn't want to delay it.

Clayton also breached the absolute blocking system. The principle of the absolute blocking system was to ensure the safe operation of a railway by allowing only one train to occupy a defined section of track at a time. This system is used on double or multiple lines where use of each line is assigned a direction of travel. Prior to the introduction of block systems, time-intervals were used to ensure that trains were spaced sufficiently apart; typically, if five minutes had passed since the first train departed then a second train was allowed to proceed, although the driver was warned that there was a train only five minutes ahead. Having cleared the Bury train to cross the viaduct he should never have granted egress to another train, even if he was certain there was no immediate danger, something he could not have known. Once the steam engine started to cross the viaduct, the deadly chain of events had begun, although there was still time to avoid a collision.

In effect, two drivers on the same track believed their paths were clear. It appears Hardman assumed two signals on the approach to the Irk Valley junction were on clear when in reality the first was actually at caution and the second, more distant, signal on danger. He should have been seen both of them. The inquest revealed that Hardman would have been able to see the caution signal for at least seventeen seconds before passing it; yet he didn't slow his train down and continued at a speed of forty miles per hour. Why he then ignored the danger signal is another mystery: he had plenty of time to stop the train, yet continued at the expected speed of a cleared train. The inquest could only make the assumption that Hardman was complacent and had assumed the signals were in his favour, as that would have been his experience in the past.

The possibility was also raised that Hardman may have fainted or even suffered a cardiac arrest, but he had been able to move towards the emergency brakes – the so-called 'dead-man's handle' – at the moment of impact. So the inquiry was left with a mystery: why did he ignore signals that could have saved his passengers? Could such an experienced train driver really have elected to assume rather than check? If so, it was an incredible error of judgement, especially for someone considered a stickler for the rules by his colleagues. If Hardman had suffered some sort of seizure, the answer could not be found in his broken body which had sustained such horrific injuries that a post-mortem was impossible.

Two other signalmen, Davenport and Upton, were apportioned some of the blame but Clayton's decision to ignore regulations and Hardman's inexplicable decision to run past the final signal were the two main factors in the crash. The inquest noted that the reasons Hardman sped towards his death would go to the grave with him. It was completely out of character for a man who was held in high esteem, had an exemplary safety record and had been in good cheer on the day of the accident. The brakes on the train also were in good working order. As Clayton survived the accident, he bore the brunt of the blame, with the investigator noting that he was inexperienced and should not have been given so much responsibility at such a young age.

As is often the case after such incidents, the Irk Valley crash brought about a number of changes and recommendations that ultimately helped rail travel become safer. If there is any consolation to be gleaned from the disaster, that is it. Today, there is a section of the viaduct wall that looks a little newer than the rest of the bridge, otherwise there is little to show there was ever a major train crash. In fact, the brickwork is the only reminder of that terrible day back in August 1953.

There is, however, a touching postscript. Fifty-seven years after the accident, in July 2010, Jeremy Halls was able to express his gratitude to the hero who saved his life. Thanks to a newspaper appeal he was put in touch with Neil Robinson, who was a 14-year-old schoolboy in August 1953. Although Jeremy's coach was submerged in the Irk, Neil noticed bubbles in the water, dived in and dragged the 6-year-old to safety. Now finally reunited the two men spent half an hour on the phone, with Jeremy saying that he was 'overwhelmed' to speak to his saviour after more than five decades had passed. Neil had also been a passenger on the train, along with his family, and while they had all survived his father's back was broken while his mother was left traumatised. Although Jeremy was then living in Wales, and Neil in Bury, they hoped that one day they would meet in person.

18

TAKE THOSE KNICKERS DOWN!

If being born within the earshot of Bow Bells means that you are a true Cockney, then anyone born within staggering distance of Tommy Ducks must surely be a true Mancunian. From 1867, this most cherished of city-centre watering holes was a meeting place for all manner of individuals, drawn by the irresistible pull of its unique charm. Numerous actors from the nearby theatres and the studios of BBC North and Granada Television would prop up its bar over the years and towards the end of its existence, tourists from around the world joined the pub's unique clientele. Thespians in particular thrived in the ribald, earthy atmosphere with the odd décor of theatrical bills and bric-a-brac setting the creative juices flowing.

There were plenty of nooks and crannies for those with familiar faces wanting no more than a quiet drink. However, those just dipping their toe into show business would revel in the opportunity to discuss future projects – a little too loudly – and name-drop liberally to impress the lesser mortals within earshot. Tommy Ducks had more than its fair share of regulars, curious students and shoppers and they kept the tills ringing for more than a century, enough for it to become part of the fabric of Manchester city centre and a much-loved landmark. The pub successfully fought closure for the best part of twenty years, somehow winning reprieves when all seemed lost as people power and sentiment-ality triumphed over bureaucracy. That is, until it literally vanished one night, causing outrage.

A pint in town would never be the same again and as one regular recalled, 'One moment it was there, the next it was gone.' During the modern era, the pub had been revered for the ladies knickers that adorned its ceiling, but after a brewery-instructed demolition team crushed Tommy Ducks in a matter of hours to make way for a new, characterless office block, the unusual decor lay scattered among rubble, broken glass and dust. Money, it seems, will always triumph over sentiment.

The main problem for Tommy Ducks was that it occupied land in the middle of a major regeneration project. With the Midland Hotel on one side and the G-Mex exhibition centre to its rear, it represented an unwanted, ageing eyesore to developers and city planners. They had pencilled in a group of buildings that would cover one million square feet in the Lower Moseley Street/Oxford Street area of town. As far back as 1972, London-based developer Heron had been planning for life without the historic venue, drawing up a blueprint for a complex of offices, housing and an entertainment centre. But the ambitious plans hit a snag when part of the targeted area came under the scrutiny of the Department of the Environment, which announced that the nearby buildings on Oxford Street were to be listed.

Brewers Greenall Whitley, the owners of Tommy Ducks, were adamant – at least publicly – that the pub would stay and amid the furore issued a statement, 'We would not be agreeable to any development that would mean losing Tommy Ducks, and we shall certainly fight to keep it.' That stance, sadly, would change as time moved on, if there ever really was a genuine objection from the brewery in the first place.

The pub's origins were of particular interest to local historians. Too many buildings had been lost as prosperity attracted new businesses to Manchester, eager to set up shop in shiny new premises. Traditionalists wanted to preserve some remnants of the past and Tommy D's fitted neatly into that category.

Originally four cottages knocked together, the pub on East Street began life as the Princes Tavern and won its first licence to serve alcohol in 1867. In a city of rough, quirky pubs it soon earned a reputation for its curious mixture of vulgarity and warmth. Landlords came and went with the less stout surviving a few weeks and those with steelier resolve staying on for years. The original name came from its proximity to the

Prince's Theatre on Oxford Street, literally a stone's throw away. A tradition was born. The actors inspired the early décor of theatrical posters and bills from across the world. Records no longer exist, but the popular story is that Thomas Duckworth, the first recorded landlord of the pub, arranged for his name to be put above the door by a hapless (but cheap) local artist. Payment was several jars of beer, but the task was not undertaken until payment had been received. Therefore, a slightly worse-for-wear sign-writer discovered Thomas Duckworth to be too much effort and instead wrote 'Tommy Ducks'. He could never have anticipated how quickly his misspelt sign was adopted and after that there was little point in calling it anything else. Tommy Ducks was perfect.

The clientele was never less than colourful throughout the pub's 125-year existence. It was a place in which off-duty detectives mixed with known crooks, vagrants popped in from local hostels to drink alongside wealthy visitors staying at the sumptuous Midland Hotel. Nobody was turned away; all were welcome. Over the years its reputation spread well beyond the city limits and it became something of a tourist destination, highlighted in guidebooks and by word-of-mouth. Once you'd drunk there, you were an honorary Mancunian.

Punters were served by street-savvy barmaids who could have walked straight off the nearby set of the Rovers Return, the fictional pub in hit soap *Coronation Street*. At various periods in time, a donkey drank at the bar (it was owned by the landlord of the day and kept in the yard) and a dog collected empty bottles at closing time – when it could muster enough enthusiasm. Most famously of all, attractive women learnt the real price of a nip in Tommy D's: donating an undergarment, preferably knickers, which would be hoisted up to hang from the ceiling.

As a result, drinkers had two hundred pairs of knickers of various sizes and colours above their heads, all adding their own unique curiosity value. From the 1960s on, it was the saucy décor that won the pub fame far and wide. Women sent in knickers from all over the world in the hope of taking pride of place on the ceiling. Incidentally, the lucky few chosen by the landlord to join this exclusive club would be asked to donate their pride and joy in exchange for a special pair of Tommy's own-brand knickers. However, certain ladies – those who had enjoyed a few too many gins – had to be dissuaded from taking off their underwear in the bar and were informed that a trip to the ladies was the rule. The pub, after all, had a reputation to protect!

Former 1970s landlord Phil Ormond, perhaps typical of the sort of character needed to run the place, recalled.

> It sometimes took me as long as an hour to talk them off, and yes I did get many refusals. Of course, if a girl looked like she was going to belt me, I moved away quickly.
>
> The only condition we had was the knickers had to be warm. One woman had the cheek to offer me a pair straight from Marks and Spencer's. She told me she'd come all the way from Kendal and looked as though she may burst into tears as a result, so I said, 'Look, love, put them on first and I'll consider adding them to the collection.'

Alas, the fate of the M&S specials remains a mystery.

Some of the nation's favourite actors would enjoy a tipple in Manchester's favourite hostelry. Count Dracula himself, Christopher Lee, popped in when he was in town, though he would always grimace when asked if he'd like a Bloody Mary. J. B. Priestley and Tommy Cooper also loved the place and there were countless others, most of whom would sign a photo recording their visit for posterity.

It wasn't all about gimmicks and star-spotting at Tommy D's, however. This was a serious drinker's venue, boasting 126 different optics, by some distance the largest selection in the city. It was possible to sample all the Irish and Scottish whiskies as well as most of the Yankee Bourbons. Ormond reckons that his open offer of £100 to anyone who could take a nip from all 126 bottles during the course of an evening was never taken up. If anyone had attempted the feat, a gravestone slab that served as a table was on hand for any poor soul foolish enough to have a go. Its inscription reads:

> *In loving memory of the skeleton in the coffin.*
> *May he rest in peace.*
> *Wherever he might be, have a drink on me.*

Prior to the gravestone, there was a glass-covered coffin containing a real skeleton, but Sixties landlord Ken Rig swapped it for a pair of piranhas, proving that where Tommy Ducks was concerned you really couldn't make it up. No wonder the punters kept coming back for more.

With a black-and-white facade, inside the pub there were brass rails, stained-glass windows, yellowing photos of Edwardian music hall artistes and flowered chamber pots on the window ledges. It was, without doubt, a preposterous jumble of nostalgia. Two porcelain toilet seats welded down as chairs could also be lifted to reveal Victorian commodes.

After 112 years of colourful life, Tommy D's was still grabbing the headlines when, in March 1979, a group of women's libbers stormed the pub to tear down the knickers from the ceiling. They distributed leaflets around the pub, claiming there were bacteria dropping into drinks and food from the knickers pinned above. Scuffles broke out as fifteen protestors fought with the regulars, causing the wife of landlord Barry Davies to cut her arm as she fell through a window. The scene was like something out of a Carry On movie.

It is doubtful if any pub would get away with that type of decor today: in addition to the underwear on the ceiling, there were nude women on calendars and pictures of topless barmaids. But in 1979 the concept of political correctness had yet to be invented. For better or worse, that was how things were back then. The women's lib incident brought national attention to Tommy Ducks, mostly because it was so bizarre. The landlord's claim that most of the garments were indeed dusty and due for a wash, did little for the pub's somewhat tarnished image.

It was a sign of things to come. With theme bars and sports pubs popping up all over Manchester, suddenly Tommy Ducks seemed out of step with the world at large. By the mid-Eighties landlady Denise Kelly had taken on the pub and as the exploitation argument rumbled on she decided she would have to be even handed between the sexes. She turned the tables by replacing some of the knickers with a collection of men's boxer shorts. 'We gave blokes a pair of our tinned knickers,' Kelly explained. 'They went into the loo, got changed and handed over their shorts. It was a lot of fun and it stopped the fights.'

Kelly had her own theory about where the tradition started. 'I believe it began when a cleaner found several pairs of knickers in a local womaniser's flat and decided to hang them in the bar. The collection was unbelievable, especially the old-fashioned ones. There were even some fur knickers!'

In March 1987, after Greenall's won planning permission for a two-storey extension in order to create a new upstairs lounge, as well as giving the old place a complete revamp, it seemed the pub would survive into the new millennium after all. The knickers weren't completely consigned to history, simply because of fierce protest from regulars, who demanded that a few mementoes from the pub's golden age were retained. Therefore, around forty pairs were housed in a special glass case on the wall.

However, the threat of demolition resurfaced again in the early 1990s. Campaigners had heard it all before and were confident they could fend off yet another attempt to destroy this famous city landmark. The Victorian Society, along with CAMRA (the Campaign For Real Ale) joined forces when they learned that Greenall's had submitted planning permission for an eleven-storey office block in November 1992. The then managing director of Greenall's, Roger Young, declared.

> We will be sorry to lose Tommy Ducks pub, which stands in the way of the proposed development. However, we recognise the importance of this redevelopment to the regeneration of this part of central Manchester and shall actively be seeking a site for a traditional quality new pub in the area.

What campaigners for the pub's preservation didn't realise was how little time they had to save their cherished establishment. Perhaps fittingly, the demise of Tommy Ducks was as rapid as its 126-year history had been dramatic. After closing time on 22 February 1993, the last drinkers were ushered out and shortly after midnight, the waiting bulldozers moved in. The destruction was swift and irreversible and by the early hours of 23 February Tommy Ducks was no more than a pile of bricks, broken glass and masonry. The decision to demolish was taken despite the fact that Manchester City Council had not yet rubber-stamped the demolition. However, rather than risk yet another protest, bosses at Greenall's decided the time was right and that it had to go, regardless of the implications. Some at the company no doubt believed that any furore would be short-lived but they underestimated the fury of the people of Manchester.

CAMRA member Peter Wadsworth recalled, 'People walked over the rubble, staring in complete disbelief. There was a real sense of loss and people were quite devastated. The glass cabinet the knickers had been displayed in was smashed under the bricks and the pub had even been open the night before.'

Greenall's, many believed, had jumped the gun. Despite the furore, planning permission was finally granted to build a nine-storey office block. The Bishopsgate Building on Lower Moseley Street was to be built opposite to the Midland Hotel with an underground car park for seventy-three vehicles, but still the memory of Tommy Ducks lived on.

The chairman of the Manchester Conservation Areas and Historic Buildings labelled the scheme, 'crude, gross and entirely inappropriate to its location. In fact, I consider this to be one of the least acceptable schemes in the city centre in the last twelve months. In an Olympic city one would have thought our standards would have been higher, not lower.'

Greenall Whitley were hauled through the courts, but ultimately fined a paltry £1,500 for the 'deliberate and wanton' demolition of Manchester's most famous pub. The brewery's response that the building was not listed or protected and that planning permission for demolition was not required.

Labour MP Bob Litherland pointed out that if the pub had sold a mouldy pie, it would have been fined £20,000. He argued: 'This exposes the weak planning laws. Unless the law is changed, Tommy Ducks won't be the last pub to vanish. It might have been flattened under the cover of darkness, but Tommy Ducks will not lie down.'

Today, the new building stands next to a dozen other new buildings, each difficult to differentiate from the next. The memory of the pub lives on following the creation of Tommy Ducks Whiskey Bar on Newton Street a few years back – with numerous whiskies to sample. It pays homage to the city-centre original. As for historic pubs in Manchester, this was the city's greatest loss and impossible to replace. From the knickers on the ceiling to a dog collecting empties, the like of Tommy Ducks will never be seen again.

More's the pity . . .

ACKNOWLEDGEMENTS

I couldn't have completed this book without the help, drive and passion of my publisher James McCarroll, whose editorial expertise and advice helped at crucial times. I can't understate his contribution on several chapters contained within and if the book is a success, it is down to his efforts.

I'd like to thank Susan and Alan from the *Manchester Evening News* archive department – both now retired, sadly – for their help and patience as I hunted down files and clippings on various stories. Their assistance was invaluable and I regret not being able to include their surnames (because I never knew for certain!)

Finally, thanks to the reporters, journalists and the people of Manchester who have all played a central role in this book, perhaps unknowingly to a certain extent, but their work, writings and words helped me cement the bricks of each story together.

FRONT-COVER PHOTOGRAPHS

Top row: *from left to right*: Jackie Brown, the Manchester Express, and the city's first boxing world champion; Feeding the giraffe at Belle Vue, the Showground of the World (© MEN Media); Pat Phoenix, then at the height of her fame for her brilliant portrayal of Elsie Tanner in *Coronation Street* (© Press Association)

Middle row: The Woolworth's fire of May 1979, one of the worst tragedies Manchester has ever experienced (© MEN Media); The great comedian and film star, Frank Randle, a true man of the North (© Mirrorpix); The Christmas Blitz of December 1940, in which Manchester city centre was devastated, although it did not weaken the resolve of the citizenry (© MEN Media)

Bottom row: Freddie Garrity, lead singer of Freddie and the Dreamers, and unlikely chart toppers in America, along with fellow Manchester bands Herman's Hermits and Wayne Fontana and the Mindbenders (© Mirrorpix); Manchester-born Robert Donat won the best-actor Oscar for his role in the 1939 movie *Goodbye Mr Chips*, showing here in the West End of London (© Getty Images); Bernard Manning, probably the most-popular, and funniest, British comedian of the 1970s, but whose later years were dogged by controversies over his jokes about race (© Mirrorpix)